GW00725674

WHAT IS TRANSACTIONAL ANALYSIS?

A PERSONAL AND PRACTICAL GUIDE

BY

ERIC WHITTON

Published by Gale Centre Publications for

THE GALE CENTRE, WHITAKERS WAY, LOUGHTON, ESSEX, IG10 1SQ.
Tel (081) 508 9344. FAX (081) 508 1240

Cover by Lizzie Spring.   ISBN: 1 870258 24 X

Published by Gale Centre Publications
Whitakers Way
Loughton, Essex
IG10 1SQ

© Gale Centre Publications, 1993

British Library Cataloguing in Publication Data

A CIP record for this book is available from the British Library

ACKNOWLEDGEMENTS

The author wishes to express his appreciation to the following authors for their permission to reprint material originally published in the *TA Bulletin* and the *TA Journal:*

The Egogram: John Dusay TAJ July 1972

The Drama Triangle: Steve Karpman TAB April 1968

The Miniscript: Taibi Kahler TAJ January 1974

The OK Corral: Franklyn Ernst TAJ April 1973

He is also grateful for the support of his colleagues during the writing of this book, for reading the drafts and making many helpful suggestions.

Most of all, he recognises how much of the material here comes from the experience of his clients and students. To them all, a big hug!

CONTENTS

PREFACE

Why a personal and practical guide?
The personal and practical guides aim to help you understand what a particular therapy is about and what it feels like to experience it and to be a therapist in it. The check lists, descriptions, exercises and case histories in the guides are designed to allow you to form an individual study programme or a study programme with a group of colleagues. This programme will not turn you into therapists nor will it enable you to work on a deep level on therapeutic problems and it is not designed with either of these aims in mind. What it will do is give you an experience of how the therapeutic method works by suggesting practical exercises you can do yourself. It will also give you an experience of what it feels like to be a therapist giving that sort of therapy, the sort of problems for which the therapy can be used to help and the likely outcome.

After this study programme you will at the very least know what the therapy is about and be able to talk coherently about it. You will also have a better idea of whether you would want to be a client in that form of therapy and whether you would want to develop an expertise in it. I also hope that experienced and practising therapists will be able to find elements in the therapies described which they will be able to use to supplement and develop their own skills.

It is generally a requirement of training as a therapist that the therapist undertake therapy. It often strikes me as odd that therapists writing about their work make only scant references to their own therapy.
Therapists seem to be particularly reticent in talking about their own therapy, yet at the same time maintain that there is no stigma attached to therapy.
Therapy is not a science, it is an art and research has shown that the individual qualities of the therapist are often more significant than the method used. It seems odd that so little writing about therapy includes the personal experiences of therapists and their difficulties and failures in therapy.

The current Green revolution and the growth of interest in alternative therapies means that we are starting to pull away from the deification of scientific objectivity. This poses a problem for psychotherapy which has for so long been trying to gain acceptance by the scientific community. In its attempt to gain respectability and distance from the parodies of the actor and cartoonist, psychotherapy has used a form of scientific research and writing which alienates therapy from its true roots which are in the arts and the social sciences and not the natural sciences.

If, as I believe, psychotherapy is a search for an answer to that most fundamental of questions "Who am I", it is as much a search for a personal morality as a cure for mental pain and psychological disease. Then there is every place for subjectivity in the process itself and in books there is a place for the personal history and the personality of the author.

Humanistic psychology tends to provide more space for human error and fallibility on the part of the therapist but even in that discipline there is not enough trust for people to really be open about themselves. In this series I have made no attempt to edit out the personal approach of the authors, far less my own personality. In fact, I have encouraged them to include their personal experiences. There are plenty of books on every method of therapy written from the so called objective viewpoint and this series is offered as a counterweight to them.

The personal and practical guides do not take part in the internecine nor the intranecine battles that proliferate in most therapies but aim to put its readers in an informed position where they can make up their own mind. I welcome feedback from readers and as the books are printed on short runs can often incorporate it in future editions.

A note on Gender: to avoid the awkwardness of phrases like him/or, he/she the male authors of the series are asked to use the words he, him, etc. while the female authors use the female pronouns.

Derek Gale.

INTRODUCTION

Transactional Analysis or TA is a simple method of describing our experience of life in such a way that both makes sense and brings a smile of recognition which gives hope for change. Eric Berne, the originator, sought to bring a positive and realistic approach to human experience. What has flowed from his original framework of thinking and practice is a wide-ranging approach to therapy.

It consists of a description of personality with three parts (*Parent-Adult-Child*); the way in which people 'set up' relationships (*Games*) and their lives generally which produce certain pay-offs based on early decisions (*Scripts*). By giving attention to what is going on between people (*Transactions*), it is possible to find other options for relating to others. It is a method of clarifying and changing the way you see yourself and interact with other people. The basic ideas of TA can be summarised in a few simple key words -

- Parent, Adult, Child - Games - Rackets - Strokes - Scripts

The idea of this book is to explain some of the pictures - mental and emotional - which are used by TA practitioners and their clients. It is not my purpose to write a definitive text book - there are a number of those - or to cover in any comprehensive way the whole TA system. There will be a number of aspects that I shall not deal with or only refer to in passing.

My purpose is to present a personal account of TA which I hope will serve as 'a plain man's guide' for those who may be considering therapy for themselves, who may have decided to look for help in dealing with their difficulties, and want to know what it is and how it works in practice - the possible benefits, advantages and limitations. At the same time, it could act as an introduction to those in helping roles who may be looking for some insights to assist them in helping people. I hope it will encourage readers to make further exploration by joining a group or attending a workshop (see list of organisers in the appendix).

So the emphasis will be practical. Each chapter has the basic ideas presented in an accessible way (in the way they have "grabbed" me) together with check lists and exercises to help you to ground the ideas in your experience. During the past twelve years I have presented TA to a variety of people - those with no previous experience of counselling, those who have read a bit, workers in the community, as well as my clients and students. In all this time I have never failed to feel excited about the dynamic of TA ideas which I think is infectious. It is my hope that this short book will convey to you, the reader, some of that quality of interest, so that you will want to learn more and use it in your personal life and work.

How did I get into TA? How has it helped me both personally and professionally?

Prior to becoming a therapist I was a trainer in education, and as part of my own professional development I participated in a number of therapy experiences in the humanistic field: Encounter, Gestalt, Bioenergetics, before deciding to undertake some extensive training in TA. I remember vividly my first introduction with Dr Mike Reddy at the Quaesitor growth centre. I had recently separated from my wife and my little boy Nicky had just died and I was feeling as though there weren't enough tears to shed. I went on the course just because it was something to do to occupy my time.

I was completely taken out of myself by my fascination with this approach to growth. Most of my experiences in therapy up to that point had been heavily emotional, usually leaving me with more to deal with than before, whereas Mike's witty, sensitive and perceptive way of working enabled me to have my feelings about all sorts of events in my life, including the death of my son, without "going up the wall". I found a new way, that suited me, of feeling and thinking about myself which helped me to make better sense of my experience.

This is in no way to denigrate the previous experiences. I think they were essential to my development and have given me an appreciation of the distinctive value of almost every methodology. No one system is good per se -

2

it is only as good as the practitioner and its effectiveness depends on whether it suits any particular individual.

Following this introduction, I went on a six month intensive course with Mike Reddy, before taking out a training contract with him. During the next three years I learned a vast amount from him and a wide range of teachers which were included as part of his training programme.

After that I continued in training and supervision with Alice Stevenson. Her approach to therapy and to life in general is generous, challenging and fun. With her I have developed skills and insights in which she has supported my natural ability and style within the framework of TA. As a teacher she has the ability to bring out the best in people. I am indebted to her and the richness of TA for bringing me years of enjoyment in working with people, and the immense satisfaction of seeing hundreds of changed lives.

For the past twelve years, I have worked as a therapist and incorporated much from other disciplines. One of the assets of TA is that it provides a framework which is amendable to almost any other approach to therapy. Muriel James in her book *Techniques in TA* gives examples of how other therapies can be used in conjunction with TA.

The aspect of TA training and practice which influenced me most was the emphasis on groups, both for supervision and therapy. I still believe that, generally speaking, they are the most effective medium for change.

In the following chapters I will describe the concepts and approaches used in TA to help people understand how they have written the "story of their lives" - the components which are common to everybody, the origins and patterns which are unique to each individual, and throughout indicating that people can change. At the close, I will show the methods used in TA to assist people to discover how they can change their story and its ending.

What is Transactional Analysis?

Transactional Analysis provides a simple method of understanding feelings and behaviour. It includes a description of personality which shows that people have three ego states, relating to patterns of behaviour. These are called Parent, Adult and Child. The Parent ego state consists of programmed attitudes and messages which come from what we heard and saw our parents doing. The Adult ego state processes information from inside us and from our environment. The Child ego state holds the feelings that we had in the past and experience in the present. Knowing the ego state we are in, enables us to change to another, more favourable state.

The way in which people relate to each other follows clear patterns, called transactions, between ego states. The way in which we transact is strongly affected by our need for strokes - the experience of being recognised - which gives us a sense of identity and worth. Games are crooked ways of getting strokes which usually result in familiar bad feelings, called rackets. When people understand how they feel and behave in a predictable way, they can recognise the early decisions they made. We can change these by re-experiencing the original feelings and make a new decision which breaks the old parent-controlled pattern.

Basically, TA is a form of therapy which, because of its clarity and versatility has been applied to a wide range of human relations training in education, social work, medicine, commerce and industry.

TA practitioners hold the following:

    1. A belief that everyone is OK - having intrinsic dignity and worth.

    2. A commitment to change.

    3. We all made self-limiting decisions in childhood which we can re-evalue and change.

4

4. The nature of this change is determined by contracts made between clients and therapists, taking shared responsibility for the outcome.

In TA therapy and counselling you will find people talking about their Parent, Adult and Child - the three distinctive parts of their personality *(ego states)* which are all available and necessary for living as a whole person. When people start to work on their problems, they soon begin to experience a recurring pattern in their lives *(their life script)*, their negative feelings and how they play games.

The therapy involves clients gaining recognition for their experience and achievements; being confronted from a caring position in the ways they are discounting themselves and others; re-experiencing in the present any relevant events in the past, to get emotional release from feelings or beliefs they may be holding on to, which are stopping them from getting their needs met now.

Although one of the aims of TA is to help people to think clearly about their difficulties, a lot of attention is given to feelings as a stimulus for action. There is a strong emphasis on change - What are you going to do, and how are you going to do it? TA is primarily a group method, emphasising that in order to change, people need support, challenge and practice with their peers.

Origines and developments of Transactional Analysis

In the early sixties there was a ferment of ideas which heralded a change in the thinking and behaviour of people all over the western world. This was a result of the questioning of long established attitudes to authority arising out of the experience of the Second World War. Together with this there was the sexual revolution and the emergence of a youth culture which found a powerful expression in pop music. This counter-culture insisted on the rights of people as individuals to decide for themselves and was accurately described as the "me" generation (over against "them").

Within this social and political change there was an increasing interest in psychology and personal development - what has been labelled the "Growth Movement". The institutional roots of psychology and psychotherapy which were firmly planted in the practice of medicine were challenged by radical psychiatrists like Thomas Szasz and Ronnie Laing who pointed our the iniquity of using psychiatry as a means of social control. Carl Rogers who pioneered client-centred therapy, Fritz Perls, the founder of gestalt therapy, Bob Schultz who popularised encounter groups and many other leading figures in the growth movement provided an "alternative" approach which challenged the paternalism of the establishment which had used its power and expertise to insist that they knew what was best for people. Most of the exponents of this change were practising in the United States and particularly in California.

Eric Berne

The most enigmatic of these was Eric Berne who lived and worked for most of his life in and around San Francisco. Eric Berne was an undoubted genius who rebelled against the establishment after he was turned down for membership of the San Francisco Psychoanalytic Institute in 1956. In 1947, after leaving the Army as a psychiatrist, he began working on his studies of intuition in which he rejected the Freudian concept of the unconscious. By the end of 1957 he had created a new approach to psychotherapy. The fruition of this work was the publication of *Transactional Analysis in Psychotherapy* in 1961.

He was a shy and secretive man with a brilliant wit and a down to earth sense of humour. He had the ability to make people chuckle as he revealed to them their hidden selves. He kept his personal life very separate from his public image. Many people found him distant and hard to get to know. He was married three times. After his second marriage to Dorothy, which lasted 15 years, he increasingly devoted himself to writing. The winter before he died he was working on six books. His weekly schedule was immensely demanding with a private practice in Carmel and San Francisco, with seminars, lectures, and psychiatric posts, although he always played poker on Friday nights.

Although Eric Berne was an eccentric and complex man who could be irritatingly argumentative, competitive and moody, I think I would have liked him if I had met him. I say this, because it is clear that he took immense interest in other people's ideas and never failed to appreciate his patients for what he had learned from them. Without the personal magnetism of Fritz Perls, he drew a large number of followers who have since become leaders of their own brands of TA: Claude Steiner, Jacqui Schiff, Bob Goulding, to mention a few.

From reading his biography I realise why he was so private. In his personal relationships he seemed to enjoy his role as a father, a husband and a friend, but he never managed to fulfil his quest for intimacy. He was devoted to his clients and followed his father's example of a human and conscientious physician. He talked about therapists being "real doctors", not purely in the medical sense, but practitioners who cured people. He had no time for the expression of negative feelings for its own sake and valued laughter as therapeutic. He was an iconoclast - the little boy who saw that the king wasn't wearing any clothes. He told a joke about the way that patients are diagnosed in the average clinic.

"The person who has less initiative than the therapist is called passive-dependent; the person who has more initiative than the therapist is called a sociopath."

He attacked sham and put-downs using a lot of big words. He invented a system of therapy based on simple words that anyone can understand. This is the spirit of Eric Berne which I salute.

Eric Berne's singular contribution was the diagram of the three ego states - distinguishing the Parent ego state from the Adult in the alive grown-up person and separate from the alive small person (the Child) in everyone. This model enabled people to see clearly what was happening inside themselves and in their transactions.

The publication of *Games People Play* (1964) which became a best seller, launched TA into the realm of pop psychology. This indicates one of the drawbacks of TA. Because you can pick up the ideas easily, it can become a slick, DIY, instant, cure-it-all. When the ideas of TA are used for personal use and problem-solving, this criticism is not so valid. "Whatever works", I am sure, would be Eric Berne's comment.

Fortunately this phase did not last and over the past 20 years TA has gradually become widely respected as a major system of psychotherapy, as well as being used extensively in education and industrial training.

WHAT IS TA?

I have come to appreciate the profound and ingenious character of TA. I never cease to be fascinated by the constant flow of ideas and research that are presented in the *TA Journal*. Some fall quickly by the wayside. But the spirit of TA is to try anything, not to reject it because at first sight it may look naïve. I don't like theories which are trying to re-invent the wheel or to expound ideas which are so complicated as to be of little practical use and which usually come with diagrams resembling electrical circuit layouts!

TA after Eric Berne

This is the title of a book edited by Graham Barnes in 1977 which brought together all the developments since Berne died. It is still a fine collection of articles by the leading TA practitioners of the time. In such a short period three major schools had emerged.

The *Classical School* represents Berne's original teaching and consists largely of those immediately associated with him in the San Francisco Seminars.

The *Cathexis School* was founded by Jacqui Schiff. The name is derived from the Institute in California which specialises in the treatment of schizophrenia. The work is based on a model of re-parenting, in which the client regresses and lives through a second childhood with new parenting from the therapist.

The *Redecision School*, originated by Bob and Mary Goulding, combines the theory of TA and the techniques of Gestalt therapy. The emphasis is on re-experiencing the original feelings which were the basis of early decisions and break through the impasse between two ego states. There is considerable emphasis on personal responsibility. Somehow or other you got into this, and somehow or other you *can* get out of it!

In addition to these developments there have been some outstanding theoretical additions to the body of TA, particularly the Miniscript of Taibi Kahler, the Racket System of Richard Erskine and Marilyn Zalcman and the Cycle of Development by Pam Levin.

The place of TA

Clearly through its originator, Eric Berne, the roots of TA lie in psychoanalysis. Since then it has moved into the humanistic field, alongside Gestalt and Client-centred Therapy. Although it has a highly developed theoretical structure, in its practice it is a lively, optimistic method of therapy. In various contexts I have seen it labelled as cognitive, analytical, behavioural. Derek Gale in the first book of this series *What is Psychotherapy* puts TA in the "in-betweenies" section. Certainly it overlaps with a number of other disciplines. And each practitioner has his own emphasis. In my contacts in the international network of TA, I have met people whose methods and ideas are varied, but who share a common view that life is essentially good and that people can change.

My own position is firmly in the Redecision school. I don't have much time for analysing transactions or hunt the games and rackets or jumping on people because they don't speak "therapese". Before people can decide to change, they have to be aware of themselves, their needs and problems. In my work, however, I do not dwell too much on insight. I move as soon as my clients are ready into the process of re-decision, which nearly always involves an emotional shift.

WHAT IS TA?

THE STORY OF YOUR LIFE

CHAPTER ONE

THE INSIDE STORY

Living in two worlds

Human beings inhabit two different and related worlds.

The inner world is the world of emotions, memories, beliefs, dreams and fantasies, the secret world of our thoughts and hopes and fears. Images of ourselves, feelings about others and our private experiences of the world live here. The outer world is the way we act out our feelings and beliefs - how we spend our time and energy both alone and with others. This is the world of roles and games, dealings and transactions. What we do depends largely on what goes on hidden inside us. Sometimes it is congruent, sometimes in conflict.

Therapy aims to help people become aware of themselves, of the real person they are inside so that what they do is experienced as choice.

Of course there is a lot of our personality which is unknown, inaccessible, unconscious and primitive. Some cultural, social and family influences are so inbred that we hardly notice them. The more we are aware of what goes on inside us, the better position we'll be in to change what we do with ourselves and how we behave with others.

The inner world

All of us experience at times an inner dialogue which has little to do with the world around us. It is, as it were, an inner world which we have secretly constructed. In it there are characters or parts of ourselves which we rarely share with others. Talking to yourself is considered the first sign of madness, but these "voices in the head" go on all the time without a sound, albeit sometimes out of our awareness.

It is one of the first tasks of TA therapy to help people get in touch with these voices, encouraging them to reveal some of their "crazy" thoughts.

"The therapeutic setting allows for a kind of craziness without the isolation that makes ordinary crazy experiences so frightening",

as Carl Whitaker puts it.

"...craziness is where life is. Life is not in social adaption. Life is the expression of one's whole self..."

It is reassuring to know almost everyone experiences a kind of craziness.

Ego states

Eric Berne called these parts of us that talk to each other Ego States, i.e. states of the self. This name was intended to make the link with Freud's concept of the "ego": the part that expresses the persona. But Berne stressed that the difference was that the Ego States are realities, not abstractions.

Assagioli, who originated psychosynthesis, extended this into what he called sub-personalities, i.e. how each client experiences these voices which have a character all of their own. Fritz Perls talks of the inner conflict as that between the "top dog" and the "under dog".

TA helps us to discover who we are with a simple but profound model:

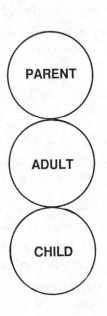

PARENT is a collection of thoughts, behaviours, attitudes and feelings, taken from outside sources who served as parent figures

ADULT is a data processor which takes in information and decides what is probably the best course of action and when to act

CHILD represents the feelings, thoughts and behaviours of childhood

These are the building blocks of TA. They represent the three people everyone carries around in their head.

Each is derived from the way we have experienced ourselves and others from the moment of birth.

The *Parent* in us is a composite of all the parental influences in our life - mainly our parents or guardians, as well as aunts, uncles, grandparents, teachers, clergy, neighbours, even people we have not met but admire in writing or films.

So the Parent is fundamentally a replica of our early parenting with later modifications from other sources. It is like a tape recorder which goes on replaying the things we were told when young, about what is supposed to be right, or good for us, and more powerfully what is wrong and bad: "Do this", "Don't do that ".

There are positive messages, about how to behave, think or feel (which may have been in conflict with our impulses) but kept us safe, healthy and nourished. However, not all the directions were given for our benefit. Often they were given to us to keep our parents comfortable.

The *Adult* is that part which has accumulated knowledge, experience and understanding about ourselves and the world at large. It learns how things work, can calculate the way to do things, is capable of using information to sort out what to do. It organises, plans, manages, thinks, predicts, memorises. It does not have anything to do with being "mature" or right. At best it serves the rest of the personality as an executive, but it needs direction.

The *Child* is the part of us that we were born with - the little boy or girl who thinks, feels, acts, talks, just the way he or she did when a child of certain age. The Child is not regarded as childish or immature (Parent words). The Child in us is not to be squashed or ignored. It is important to value this part as it is creative, spontaneous, clever and loving. I agree with Eric Berne that it is the best part of the personality. Sometimes it will be difficult to deal with because of bad experiences which have not been sorted out. We experience the Child mainly through our feelings, needs and desires.

When we look more closely at this inner world structure, we can see the way we have internalised so much of what we perceived externally when we were young. Later we will show how we have interpreted all of this to write the "story of our lives" (Chapter Three on scripts).

As a little baby, we only had a Child ego state. (Not until later, in adolescence, when we were able to think rationally and take care of ourselves, did we develop an Adult and a Parent.) Nevertheless, we did have a mini-Adult (A_i) and a mini-Parent(P_i) inside us, alongside a bundle of body sensations (C_i).

How we adapted when we were little

Baby Jo likes making a noise, but Mummy keeps saying "shush", so she keeps quiet, and learns not to make a fuss.

Baby Jim may need to be held, but Mummy is always too busy, so he yells and then she comes and picks him up.

In both cases they figure out: "That's the way to do it!"

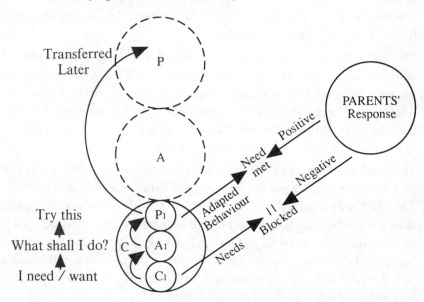

The Child in the CHILD (C_i) is the original unique infant with sensations, feelings, bodily needs and stored memories of the early years.

The LITTLE PROFESSOR (A_i) is the embryonic Adult ego state; the intuitive, resourceful part that figured out how to get the best out of any situation

The Parent in the CHILD (P_i) is our response to what was happening to us when we were small, which in later years gets transposed into the grown-up Parent ego state.

To the young child its parents are all-powerful sources of life, nurture and knowledge. Children instinctively believe that their parents will meet their basic needs. When the parenting goes wrong for any reason, the child has to adapt in the best way he can. What he doesn't know is that some of his parents' responses come from their unmet (Child) needs. The infant believes that whatever his parents do is right, even if it's bad for him. He is unable to judge when they are responding inappropriately from the Child Ego State, rather than Adult or Parent. The infant can take on these messages or rebel against them - eventually incorporating them into his own Parent ego state. These early decisions are made by the Little Professor, and in therapy this part of the person can change so as to enable him to make a free choice in adult life.

The importance of the Parent ego state

Good parenting is directed at the well-being of children. Bad parenting stems from the parent's unmet emotional needs (Child) or ignorance (Adult). So the Parent ego state is a mixture of the good and bad messages from childhood. This is open to change in adult life through new information (Adult) or our emotional discomfort (Child) from the way we have adapted. This revision of the Parent is fundamental to any change.

The Parent ego state is also open to change in adult life through new information (Adult) or emotional discomfort (Child) in the present. In later life this is fundamental to any change.

When I am working with people, it is nearly always the lack of a good internal Parent that makes it hard for them to change. They have a mean, hard or indulgent Parent that prevents their Child from having fun, satisfaction or getting on with what is important.

Parent interview

One of the techniques used in TA to change the content of a person's Parent ego state is to set up a dialogue with the client taking the role of the parent in question. This is a piece of therapy in which the client's problem happens to be a sexual issue. Yours may be about something different.

ANGELA is a client who has squashed her sexual feelings and has realised that she did this to look after her mother's fears. I asked Angela to be her mother (Maureen) so that she could become aware of how she had incorporated her mother's problem into her Parent ego state.

THERAPIST: "Well Maureen, you've heard how difficult Angela found your strictness when she was young. She thinks that you were very harsh, what do you think?"

MAUREEN *(Angela's mother)*: "I only did it for her own good. She would have got into awful trouble if I'd been easy on her."

THERAPIST: "So you didn't trust her?"

MAUREEN: "She's a good girl, but those boys ..."

THERAPIST: "What are they like? Did you have trouble with them when you were young?"

MAUREEN: "No. It was my father, who was so strict, he never let me go out in the evenings, and at weekends insisted on knowing my every movement. He used to give me lectures about getting into trouble with boys."

THERAPIST: "So you grew up frightened that boys would get you into trouble?"

MAUREEN: "Yes. I believed that there was something wrong with my feeling attracted to boys."

THERAPIST: "Can you see now that isn't true and that you have passed on your fears to Angela?"

MAUREEN: "Yes and I realise how envious I was of her having more freedom than me."

The therapist now gets Angela to be herself again. She now knows that she doesn't need to repress her sexual feelings as a way of looking after her mother's fears.

the hidden influence

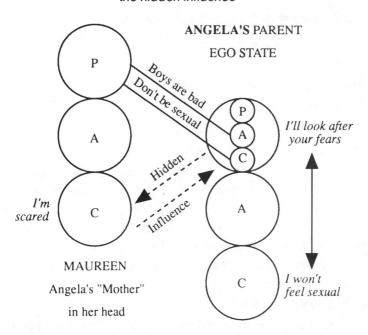

ANGELA'S PARENT

EGO STATE

P

Boys are bad
Don't be sexual

P
A
C

I'll look after your fears

A

Hidden
Influence

I'm scared

C

A

MAUREEN

Angela's "Mother"

in her head

C

I won't feel sexual

All the time in this piece of therapy the client is playing her mother and experiences what she believed the oppression was all about. It doesn't matter if it was true. Here we are only concerned with the emotional history, which is the truth for Angela, i.e. the Parent in her head tells her that there was something bad about her sexuality, so she shuts down on it to "take care" of her mother's vulnerability: the Child in her Parent ego state which was the hidden influence of her mother's Child fear.

EXERCISE TO HELP YOU TO IDENTIFY YOUR EGO STATES

Write down six words or phrases to describe yourself. Then check to see whether they describe Parent, Adult or Child characteristics.

EXAMPLE:

Jack's six words are:	Likely Ego State:
Helpful	*Parent*
Thoughtful	*Adult*
Discerning	*Parent*
Organised	*Adult*
Stubborn	*Child*
Honest	*Adult*

From this you can see that Jack sees himself mostly in Adult and least in Child. This is meant to be a rough guide, not a definitive description. That's why I put "likely" ego state. Parent words are caring or controlling; Adult words involve thinking and Child words are based in feelings (Note that here Child does not mean childish). Now see what your list looks like to you.

You can go one step further and get a friend, partner or colleague to write down words or phrases to describe you. Then you can compare your own inside picture with how you appear to others.

This will give you some practice in differentiating the three basic ego states.

When you have done this, choose three words to describe your mother and three words to describe your father. Compare them with the six words you chose for yourself. In what ways do you think you are like your father or mother?

You will now have some clues about how your ego states were formed.

From these clues you're beginning to build up a picture of the content of your ego states. You are able to recognise how your internal world is derived from the world you grew up in, and how you relate (half consciously) to the external world in the present on the basis of your past experience.

Confusions, missing parts and blind spots

What we experience inside - the voices of our ego states - influence the way we behave. Over a period of time we can deduce what is going on inside ourselves using the models below. When we are in one of these distortions, we are not always aware of what is happening, except indirectly when the response we get from others is not what we expected. Distorted ego states are contaminations, boundary problems and exclusions.

Contamination

Sometimes we distort reality because one ego state is overlapping another. This is called *contamination*:

When we mix up feelings with control. This is the source of confusion, like when I blame you when I am angry, and say "How can you leave me feeling like this?" Here I could say from my Adult "I am angry and I want to be heard". I fear you won't hear me so my fear, which is in my Child, tries to force you to stay by making you feel guilty.

When we are judging what is true through our beliefs. This is the source of prejudice. What I believe is not necessarily true: you let me down and I think "Just like men!" rather than face the fact that this man has not met my expectations and feel the disappointment.

When we are seeing the world through our feelings. This is the source of delusion, as in: I wake up feeling low, a lot of jobs to do. I'm late for work and my colleague is off ill. By the end of the day I'm thinking "The world is against me". Instead I could just recognise that this has been a bad day.

It is important that we maintain a clear distinction between our ego states so that we do not confuse what we feel in Child with what we believe in Parent with Adult reality. We need to be clear where we are coming from in order to relate effectively with others. This process of separation is often done in the early stages of therapy by setting up Three Chair work with the client experiencing his Parent, Adult and Child in each position.

Boundary issues

Lax boundaries

Sometimes people move so quickly from one ego state to another that you can hardly keep up with them. One minute they are expressing feelings, the next minute they have switched to telling someone off, and before you know where you are they are talking very factually about something, like: "I am really upset that I missed the film.", "It's all your fault. You're always late.". "It will be on next week, we can go then."

Rigid Boundaries

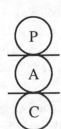

Quite often people are unaware of the other parts of themselves and get stuck in one ego state to the extent that the other two ego states are hardly active. When people stay in one ego state for any undue length of time, we notice that:

If they are stuck in Parent, they can be irritatingly helpful or over-critical, e.g. a nurse always looks after others without thinking or feeling his own needs (Constant Parent).

If people are stuck in Adult, they nearly always intellectualise events or rationalise their feelings: a boffin-like person walks into the office and describes an awful road accident in a detached manner without apparent feelings (Constant Adult).

If people are stuck in Child they tend to be over-emotional and don't think about what they are doing or care what others feel: John McEnroe gets into rages not realising the force of his behaviour (Constant Child).

The constant ego state acts like a magnet to most of their experience.

Exclusions

In contrast to constant ego states, you may notice that one ego state doesn't function a lot of the time.

When we don't use our Parent ego state, we are uncaring or controlling. This is called *Excluded Parent.*

When we don't use our Adult ego state, we stop thinking about what's happening. This is called *Excluded Adult.*

When we don't use our Child ego state, we are not expressing feelings or needs. This is called *Excluded Child.*

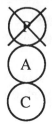      

Excluded Parent   *Excluded Adult*   *Excluded Child*

It may help to look at some extreme cases of Exclusion to see how they work.

When a person excludes Parent, he is likely to behave irresponsibly without conscience. We can see the effects of this in terrorism, addiction, when people do what they want (Child) and can organise themselves accordingly (Adult) but they have rejected their Parent who might care about the consequences.

When someone excludes Adult, he is in a state of constant confusion or conflict. He switches to and from Parent and Child, out of touch with Adult reality. The manic-depressive swings from almost complete helpless withdrawal when his oppressive internal Parent dominates, to going over the top becoming the life of the party or recklessly spending. Many great artists have suffered from this condition, their work often being the outpouring of their internal conflict.

When a person excludes Child, it means that his feelings are too painful, so he takes on responsibility for others' feelings and doesn't have fun. This is usually the result of some earlier experience when expression of feelings was punished, or when what was happening was too bad to allow feelings. Jane was raised in a strict convent school which was so painful she has forgotten what it was like. Now she is fifty, she works long hours in a hospice, never had a close relationship, rarely smiles; she spends her spare time at Samaritans and is about to complete a PhD at the Open University. Her only holidays are with her ageing parents.

When this is a common pattern of behaviour and one ego state is consistently excluded, another ego state has to take up the surplus energy, do double duty to compensate for the 'lazy' one. e.g. a person who is unexpressive of emotions (Child) may spend a lot of time instead looking after or controlling others (Parent).

The part which is inactive and needs developing is not available, so in therapy we have to deal with the active part until the client feels the discomfort of his Parent, Adult or Child working overtime.

No-one experiences a complete exclusion of an ego state. We are looking at a condition in which people spend most of their time, coming out for remission on special occasions.

CHAPTER TWO

TELLING THE STORY

Having explored the "inside story", we will see how the story unfolds in relation to the world outside of ourselves. We tell our story in the present by the way we use the parts of ourselves in transactions, the way we value people, the way we express feelings, and in the games we play.

The outer world

When we have learned to recognise the different ego states which we experience internally, we can see how they function when we relate to others. How we behave differs, not only in relation to what's going on outside, but also depending on which ego state is active in us. For a lot of the time we are making choices based on the dialogues going on inside our heads. There is a constant flow between what we experience inside ourselves and what we do.

Sometimes what I do fits with what I am experiencing inside me.

I have a feeling and express it

I tell you that I am annoyed by the noise of your radio.

I hear a message in my head which says "Don't bother other people" and so I keep my needs to myself.

I don't ask for help when I am lost in a strange town.

Sometimes the way I behave does not fit with what I am experiencing inside.

I have a feeling and express a thought instead

I am very upset when my friend tells me he has AIDS and I find myself saying "You're the third person I know with AIDS."

I hear a voice in my head saying "Make sure you work hard" and I choose to have a good time.

There's a lot of jobs to be done but I spend the evening in the pub with my mates.

The "inside story" is concerned with *what* is happening, the content of what we are experiencing inside ourselves, *what* we are thinking, feeling, valuing.

The *how* of our personality is what we do in relation to others and the world, *how* we behave in the "outer world", *how* we are seen/experienced by others.

We can observe the way in which our energy changes from one ego state to another. In relationships we express ourselves in five ways

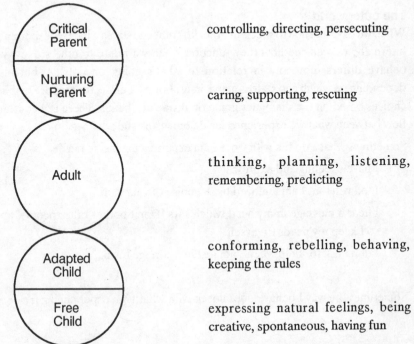

Critical Parent	controlling, directing, persecuting
Nurturing Parent	caring, supporting, rescuing
Adult	thinking, planning, listening, remembering, predicting
Adapted Child	conforming, rebelling, behaving, keeping the rules
Free Child	expressing natural feelings, being creative, spontaneous, having fun

Any of these ways of expressing ourselves can be positive or negative in terms of our own or others' well-being

Egograms

Here's a way, invented by Jack Dusay, to discover what kind of person you are by the way you use your ego states. Look at the way you spend your time and energy with others in your life and remember that this exercise is specifically about what you *do* in relation to other people, not what you *feel*.

CRITICAL PARENT: How often do you tell other people off, control or direct them?

NURTURING PARENT: How much time do you spend looking after people?

ADULT: What proportion of your time do you spend with others discussing issues or organising things?

ADAPTED CHILD: To what extent do you conform to others or rebel?

FREE CHILD: To what extent do you enjoy yourself, express your feelings, know what you want and are able to please yourself when you are with other people?

You might find it easier to plot these over the past week, for example.

In the following example, most of my time is spent in Adult and the least in Critical Parent.

CP   Little - directions to students and clients. Have a go at builders and people who are clearly not keeping agreements.

NP   I provide a lot of care for people, I listen and help when I can.

A   I discuss with people a lot. Meet to plan, get jobs done

FC   I spend my time with people in a way that pleases me. I am always looking for the funny side of things. And usually say what I feel.

AC   I like to go along with people at times, but not as a rule.

Now have a rough shot at giving yourself a score out of ten for each of the ego states and mark it on the chart below to represent the amount of time you spend in each ego state.

Now draw your egogram.

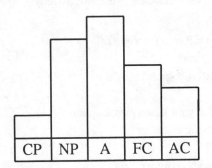 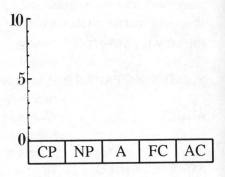

Notice the different levels you have drawn. In which ego state do you spend the most/least time? Are you more critical than nurturing in your Parent? Are you more adapted than free in your Child? Does this profile fit your lifestyle, occupation or personal life?

Transactions

A transaction consists of a stimulus and a response. There is quite a different quality to the various types of transactions, as you can see from the following:

Transactions between

Nurturing Parent / Free Child are warm and nourishing.

"Let me give you a hug"

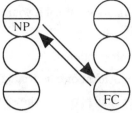

"Yes, I'd like that"

Critical Parent/Free Child are distant, uncomfortable, conflicting, demanding

"Behave yourself"

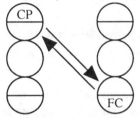

"Buzz off!".

Adult / Adult are interesting, productive, sometimes boring.

*"Have you heard the
cricket score?"*

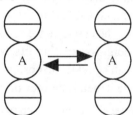

*"Yes, what do you think
of our chances?"*

Free Child / Free Child are fun, lively, competitive.

"What a fabulous car!"

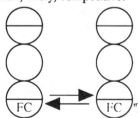

"Yea. Let's go for a spin,"

and so on ...

How about you think up some examples of your own?

Jot down a few familiar exchanges you have with people.

What do you say? What is their response?

Or what does the other person say? What is your response?

Is it Parental - nurturing or critical?

Is it Adult - questioning / informational?

Is it Child - free feeling, enjoyment or conforming, rebellious?

Then draw three circles for each person as shown below and put arrows to and from the ego states involved.

When you are acting in one ego state it doesn't mean that the others are not operating. The other ego states are active internally, sometimes out of awareness.

For example, you may be looking after someone *(Nurturing Parent)* and at the same time feeling resentful, although you are not expressing it *(Adapted Child)*. Internally you may be experiencing a conflict between your Parent and your Child. You may however decide *(Adult)* to set aside your feelings and get on with caring. We can change the ego state we use according to the person and situation we are addressing. When this fits, we are congruent and feel comfortable. When we use an ego state inappropriately, we are uncomfortable. Choosing the right ego state depends on your purpose or needs.

When you go shopping, generally it helps to be polite and clear *(Adapted Child + Adult)*. If you get bad service, you may need to be a bit angry and assertive *(Free Child + Critical Parent)* in order to get what you want.

Complementary transactions

When things are going well in relationships, I am getting the responses I want and so are you. I can change ego states and so can you so that we remain in complementary transactions. We are in harmony and communication is easy. I aim for one of your ego states and you respond accordingly:

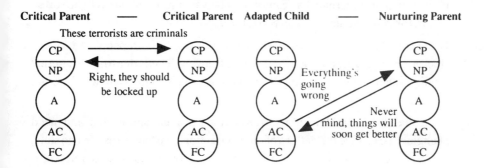

Critical Parent — Critical Parent   **Adapted Child — Nurturing Parent**

These terrorists are criminals

Right, they should be locked up

Everything's going wrong

Never mind, things will soon get better

Crossed transactions

At times the complementary response doesn't fit. I don't like being put in the ego state you want me to be, so I respond from an unexpected part of me.

It's about time you bought yourself a watch!

What's the time?

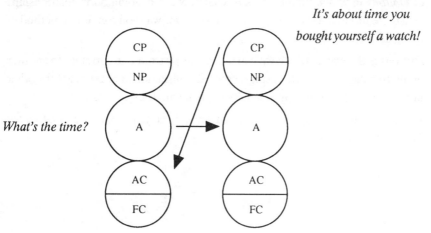

Whoops! Something's gone wrong. The subject has changed.

We are no longer talking about the time, but "Who's looking after who round here?" And until that question is resolved, communication cannot be restored.

You know immediately when you have been crossed transactionally - you feel a jerk, the conversation stops, either momentarily or completely. One or both turns away or goes off in a huff. Although this is experienced negatively, it is an indication that something has gone wrong between you, and needs to be sorted out, before communication can be restored.

Often relationships are unsatisfactory because one or both people are rigidly stuck in one ego state and can't find a way of moving. This is due to some internal rigidity, inner belief or feeling from the past. "This is the only way," we tell ourselves.

Some habitual complementary transactions are uncomfortable and need changing. To change the pattern of our transactions, we have to use an ego state, which causes enough discomfort for the other person to deal with us differently.

Options

Stephen Karpman, one of Eric Berne's early associates, came up with the idea of *Options* in which the object is to change what is going on in relationships which are unsatisfactory and get free in whatever way you can. It is a method of being assertive.

Options is the way in which we can move energy from one ego state to another in relationships. It requires using a crossed transaction in order to get the other person to relate differently, if necessary, from another ego state.

Bill is constantly demanding attention from or wants to be looked after *(Adapted Child)* by his wife Sylvia.

For example, he says regularly:

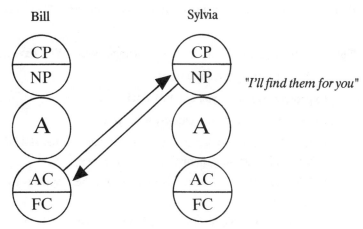

Bill

Sylvia

"I'll find them for you"

"I've lost my car keys"

The expected response is from Sylvia's Nurturing Parent. Consistently she has obliged by telling him or finding the keys. Now she wants out of that role, so she needs to shift responsibility by using another ego state, for example:

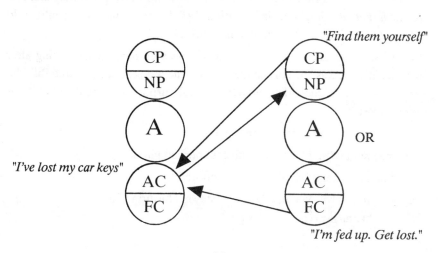

Bill

Sylvia

"Find them yourself"

"I've lost my car keys"

OR

"I'm fed up. Get lost."

Using Adult in this situation may not be strong enough to do more than slow things down, e.g. "What do you want me to do about that?" or "I'm busy".

These are the permissions you need for using options. You have a right:

to demand straight transactions

to protect yourself - you can talk back

to express yourself - you can say what you feel

to learn and use all your ego states - you can become skilled by watching others and practising them

to see how others use their ego states and their options to change their transactions

In therapy we get people to practice using other parts of themselves which are unfamiliar. At first this feels like acting, but after a time, when the client experiences the good effects in his life, it becomes more natural.

Check out in a familiar situation that you find uncomfortable, which ego state you tend to favour.

What is your usual response to your child, friend, colleague or partner?

Now ask yourself: Is it taking care of them *(Nurturing Parent)* or telling them off *(Critical Parent)* or giving information *(Adult)* or doing what you're told *(Adapted Child)* or letting out feelings *(Free Child)*?

Sylvia's was Nurturing Parent. She has always seen her role as looking after practicalities. It was hard to change because she was scared of hurting Bill who might reject her if she didn't serve that useful purpose. But she decided it was worth the risk.

What stops you from using another ego state?

You may not be used to it. You may feel pushed into it.

Now imagine using each of the other ego states.

Suppose, like Sylvia, you nearly always stay in Nurturing Parent when someone has a problem.

Now try Critical Parent - give a direction, tell them off.

Now try Adapted Child - pleasing or rebelling without helping.

Then Adult - give some information about you, the other person or the situation. Sometimes changing the subject can work.

Now Free Child - express your feelings, make a joke, sing a song.

It can be fun thinking about all sorts of unlikely responses in order to give yourself some permission to do it differently. If it doesn't work the first time, do something else. You're important. Don't give up on yourself.

Ulterior transactions

This occurs when people are not doing or saying what they mean.

There is a social transaction *and* a hidden or emotional transaction.

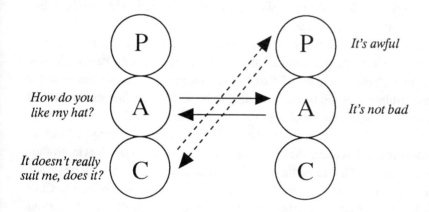

On the surface ulterior transactions are meant to get a good response, but usually hook people into doing something they don't want.

A lot of transactions have a secret meaning which is understood by both parties, but usually they are meant to manipulate and are used frequently for financial or sexual advantage.

All sorts of behaviours have hidden meanings - being late, doing shoddy work, forgetting important tasks, making put-down jokes.

Ulterior transactions are the basis for playing Games which we will deal with later in this chapter.

How can this help you?

You will be able to recognise the different ways in which you relate and shed some light on those moments of puzzlement when you see that what you are doing is not what you thought it was. You will be able to recognise how coming from one ego state has quite a different effect from another - both on you and the people you are with. Stop playing Parent when you're trying to have fun. Giving yourself a hard time (from your Critical Parent) will ensure you don't feel good for long, no matter how clever or industrious you are. In close relationships, it is helpful to realise that the intrusion of Critical Parent will spoil enjoyment. You need to be in Free Child to have the pleasure of intimate sexual relationships. You will be more exciting to be with. In dealing with important tasks while under emotional pressure, hassles can be avoided if you get some nurture for your Child, so that you can think and act more clearly in Adult. In social contexts, it is useful in any strategy for change to recognise that motivation comes from Child, finding the facts from Adult, and that asserting rights and injustice needs Parent. In staff meetings, it is important to distinguish Child needs from Adult information, so that they can be dealt with, by getting agreement about goals and options. In career development, egograms can be studied to find better fits between the person and the job.

Strokes

Strokes is the key concept which links together much of the theory of TA.

A stroke is the way in which we give and receive recognition, value or worth to one another. Any transaction can be a stroke but usually it carries with it some physical sensation of well-being.

We all know what it feels like to be stroked - touched - physically, mentally or emotionally. From the beginning of our lives, it was touch or contact which made us aware of both our existence and our worth. As we grew up, we got recognised in various ways. When we didn't, we found means of getting some attention - by pleasing or annoying others.

In our culture, strokes from touch are largely replaced in adult life by words and looks. We all need them. According to Eric Berne we would shrivel up without them.

There are strokes for doing things (conditional): "That's a good piece of work", "You play the piano well".

There are strokes for being you (unconditional): "I like you", "You have a lot of charm".

We need both kinds to stay OK. It is important though, not to confuse them. For a long time I believed that I would be loved for my achievements.

Plastic strokes are used for manipulation, flattery or phoney selling and are not genuine. Strokes can be positive or negative.

We exchange a lot of ritualistic strokes from greetings such as: "Hello, how are you?" when we meet people and from good wishes sent in birthday and Christmas cards. Maintenance strokes are those we get from everyday transactions such as when we go shopping, book tickets, as we are served in restaurants, bars, hotels etc. It is important that we know that these are constantly available, especially when we are going through a bad time. Compulsive spending and drinking can be a form of self-stroking which can have bad effects when they become a substitute for personal contact.

Then there are strokes from acquaintances, work mates, fellow travellers. Quite often, when people retire from work, a whole series of regular strokes dry up which is hard to replace.

Strokes from people who have status socially or at work carry a lot of power and are highly sought after by most people. Being complimented or noticed by those who are important to us makes us feel good in a very distinctive way. The way we exchange strokes with close friends, relatives, partners has a special quality which brings a sense of belonging and intimacy.

In addition, what you get stroked for is important. For some people hearing "You look good" is much more satisfying than "You're clever" and vice versa.

Do you get the strokes you want? The way we conduct our lives attracts certain sorts of strokes. In writing this book I notice that I am collecting lots of strokes from friends and colleagues which I value immensely. This is vital to me as writing, even in the pleasant environment of my study is a solitary occupation with a shortage of external strokes.

This brings me nicely to the experience of internal stroking which comes from inanimate objects like the sun shining into my room, the sight of the ash tree in my garden against the blue sky, or from the vast collection of strokes from my memories, ideas and fantasies. When I am working on my own and I stop writing, have a snack or listen to music, I am into self-stroking. In fact, any way that I nurture myself provides an enormous range of satisfactions. But without the regular contact with my friends, neighbours and colleagues, this source of strokes would not be satisfying for long.

Self-stroking fantasy

Think of someone who you regard as an ideal parent, the sort of parent you'd have wished for. This could be a real person you know, someone you know of from a book or a film or someone you've invented. Someone who loves and understands you. Now imagine you are sitting alone in a room and that your ideal parent has come in to be with you and giving you attention. Think of something you've always wanted. Ask your "parent" to give you what you want - to do or say something that will make you feel good. Then create a picture of that person giving you what you desire and notice how you feel. If you found this difficult, check at each stage what stopped you getting the strokes you need.

Each of us has a "screening" system for letting in and excluding certain strokes - the way we give and receive strokes may contain a filter. "Don't praise her, she'll get a big head", "Those that ask, don't get". Some people allow for more negative than positive strokes and consequently have to distort good ones. "You are very creative" changes to "She thinks I'm boring". One person I know who is very attractive and resourceful is admired by all her friends and yet complains that she never gets enough attention. She is "stroke-proof", resistant, which comes from her mother overstroking her. She would give her a prize for coming tenth in the three-legged race at school! She needs ten strokes before she feels one.

Stroking is the lynch pin of our life decisions, mode of relating, inside feelings, and personality type. On the basis of how we were given recognition when we were young, the parts of our personality got developed.

Which ego state do you use most? (refer back to your egogram on page 28)

A person who got stroked for caring will have a well developed Parent. One who got a lot of respect for thinking or organising will develop a strong Adult. If you were encouraged in doing things that were enjoyable, you will have an active Child.

In addition to the abilities you possess, a major factor in your choice of occupation is most likely derived from the aspects of your personality that got most strokes in early life. This is one of the reasons many people are doing jobs they don't like. They are still accepting a second-hand value of the way they get strokes. Quite often my clients and students become aware that they no longer want to be stroked for being self-sacrificing or doing impersonal work. Part of the therapy is the discovery that they can change their work. The relief and satisfaction they feel affects the rest of their lives.

Important life experiences such as education, sex, career, marriage, having children, money, work, holidays, joining groups, illness, addiction, age, bereavement - form the basis for a lot of direct and indirect sources of strokes.

It is worth reviewing them and the decisions you make about such things as to how you use them to support or deny your need for strokes.

EXERCISES IN GROUPS

Divide the group into threes. In each sub-group of three, two members give positive strokes to the third member for a few minutes. This is done by saying what you like about the person - looks, characteristics, abilities, activities, manner, etc. Then the person who has been receiving strokes takes a few minutes to describe that experience. Did he accept what was given? Notice any discounts.

Then move on to the second and the third person as above, so that all get strokes from the others.

A variation is to get each person to *ask* for a stroke from the others - something you want them to do or say that will make you feel good.

You can do either of these exercises in a larger group.

Each person takes a turn to sit in the hot seat and invites strokes from anyone for three minutes.

Rules for stroking - the cure for lovelessness

1. Give strokes when you have them to give

   e.g. When you feel good about someone you meet, tell him

2. Ask for strokes when you need them

   e.g. You're feeling low, pick up the phone to someone you know and ask him to listen to you or take you out, or whatever you want

3. Accept strokes if you want them

   e.g. When someone says "I like your smile", if that's something you want to be told, say "Thanks, I feel good."

4. Reject strokes when you don't want them

   e.g. When someone says "You're so good at fixing things", and you feel some manipulation, say something like "I'd rather not be told that, thanks, I'm looking for some help myself right now".

5. Give yourself strokes

> e.g. When you've done something well, tell yourself or give yourself a treat. Look in the mirror and say "I really like you / your ..."

> When you're alone and down, tell yourself "I'll look after you" and then find something pleasurable or nourishing to do.

The happy person knows that he can and will and how to get strokes.

The unhappy person believes they are limited, people are stingy, they must be equally exchanged

Some people believe that it is better to get negative strokes than no strokes at all. This may have been true when we were tiny because the worst thing then was to be abandoned. So if good strokes were not very plentiful, then without some contact we could lose any sense of our existence.

In adult life, however, this is not true. We are not dependent like that. If we refuse bad strokes (*Kicks*), at least that gives us some space to consider how to get good ones. If we cannot bear to be alone, we may develop an appetite for unhealthy strokings, as a way to ease our fears. When someone does something outrageous and gets arrested or punished in some way, it is called "attention seeking" which although it is a put-down of a person's dilemma, has a lot of truth in it - it may be the only, desperate way he knows to get strokes.

Stroking profile

It can be helpful to develop a picture of how you obtain strokes, in order to find ways of increasing them. To do this, make a list of all the things you think you get strokes for - aspects of your personality, in the way you behave or relate to others, the sort of work you do, how you spend your time. Here's an example. Fred gets strokes for being helpful, reliable, friendly, hardworking and quiet.

> How do you get strokes - by waiting for them or asking for them?

> Who do you get them from?

> What different values do they have from different people? (see chart on page 42)

What type of strokes do you get - conditional, unconditional, verbal, physical, financial, positive or negative?

Now make a list of all the things you would like to be stroked for. Some may be the same as the first list, but you may discover, like Fred, that you want people to notice the colour of your eyes!

We all have our own favoured source of strokes.

A glance from *him* or *her* is worth a thousand words from anyone else.

Praise from someone you respect.

A kiss from an admirer.

A compliment from a complete stranger.

Check during the past day/week/month the rating you give to the people you've been with ... the volume of strokes ... and make a total. Here is an example to demonstrate a method for making a Stroke Inventory:-

Monday   **Tuesday etc**

People	Rating	No Received	No. Given	Total
Colleague	50	10	0	500/0
Friend(s)	100	7	10	700/1000
Partner	500	21	7	1500/350
Shop Asst	10	3	1	30/10
Casual	5	6	5	30/25
Neighbour	10	2	6	20/60
TOTALS		49	29	

Make your own chart and see how you might improve the quality of your relationships. Getting and giving strokes is a simple and effective way to change how you think and feel about your life. There is an inexhaustible source of strokes around you. You can get them directly by asking for things. Rarely do people give an outright "No". Often they say it was nice to be asked. Then there are the multitude of indirect strokes from just talking to people, getting attention in shops; even complaining can bring some good results. Then the way you present yourself will attract strokes. For example, if you dress well, people are more likely to give you a compliment than if you appear a mess. The worst thing to do is to sit around waiting for something. You may be lucky. Watch how you limit yourself with "if onlys". Notice how you can enhance the possibilities by your need for strokes and your willingness to take risks.

EXERCISE

Make an experiment this week - to increase your stroke count.

Consider how you want to change the way you exchange strokes.

Start by giving ten free strokes to people you meet.

Collect ten extra strokes this week from people you don't usually consider.

For example

Ask for help whenever you want it.

Phone up an old friend or relative you haven't talked to for a while.

Go into a shop and ask to see the most desirable items.

Ask a new friend to tell you something good about you.

Join a new group.

Notice how you change your picture of yourself in doing different things like this.

How games, rackets and lifescripts are based on a need for strokes

In the following sections we will be looking at the various ways in which we set up our lives based on certain beliefs about ourselves. Therefore changing our stroking patterns is essential if we want to feel good, relate well and have a sense of worth about our lives.

We can use negative feelings to get strokes for being hard done by, panicky, guilty or despairing, based on the belief in the words of the song "you only love me when it rains". We can stay in one sort of familiar feeling *(Racket)* to manipulate people to give us strokes - sympathy or oppression. It is sad when we think we have to feel bad in order to get attention.

How we set up relationships *(Games)* and end up with bad feelings which "prove" our lack of self-worth or that others are bad, will reveal a lot about our need for strokes. The reason we are attracted to certain sorts of people and not to others is the belief that we will get the strokes we "deserve".

The life plan *(Script)* we have invented is derived from what we believe about ourselves - what we will get stroked for and how we procure them, even whether we will get them at all under certain circumstances.

If we find ways of getting plenty of positive strokes, we will give up seeking for strokes through bad experiences. One of the features of TA is that people have permission to give, receive and ask for strokes, on the basis that if we are to change, our stroking pattern will change. Changing is not easy, and we need all the encouragement we can get. Anyway, exchanging strokes is worthwhile for its own sake!

Feelings and rackets

In TA we distinguish between "real" feelings and racket feelings.

Real feelings are those which are a spontaneous response to what is happening in the present.

Anger, Sadness, Fear, Gladness are the four basic feelings which are:

- a stimulus for action

- a signalling system when something needs attention

- a means of solving problems

They are usually short-lived when we deal with the discomfort they produce. When I am aware of feeling angry, sad or scared, I can choose what to do about it.

I may decide to just have the feeling and let it go

I may go one step further and express what I am feeling

I may decide to report the feeling to someone

Or I can do something about it - tell someone what I want - ask for something - and then, when I have done all I can or wish to, move on.

In contrast, racket feelings, though they may be stimulated by something in the present, are usually a response related to the past. They have the following characteristics:

1. Inappropriate - Someone treads on my foot and I say "Sorry" (guilt)

2. Substitutive - Someone is rude to me and I get scared rather than angry and I smile

3. Repetitive - whenever I am faced with parting, I panic (I'm not sad)

4. Manipulative - I am miserable in order to get strokes

5. Body related - Constant frustration gives me headaches

Unlike real feelings, racket feelings can hang around for a long time, especially if I am getting stroked for them. They do not contribute to solving the problem. In fact they persist to avoid dealing with the situation. If I am feeling miserable *(racket)* and someone gives me a hug, it is likely that I will go on feeling bad or feel bad soon after - and still needy (see 4 above).

In contrast, if someone comforts me when I am feeling sad about some loss, I will feel some relief.

When we set up a racket feeling to get attention from people, we will continue to have transactions based on the position we adopt (I'm not OK or You're not OK). The racket is the process we learned in childhood: we have to feel bad in a certain way in order to get strokes.

Although any feeling can be rackety, there are some emotional states which are clearly based on a picture of ourselves which is not true or which stop us from doing something and getting on, like helplessness, inadequacy, embarrassment, depression, anxiety, desperation, confusion, misery, feeling cornered, disgust.

We all have our "favourite" feeling, when things go wrong. We always get angry, or we don't have to wait too long before we feel panicky. They are feeling states which cling to us like treacle. We find it hard to shake them off because we are stuck in an impasse of childhood.

Depending upon your racket, you may react differently from others in the same situation. When there's a delayed flight, some feel outrage, some resignation, some panic, some depressed - and there will most likely be a statement said or unsaid to go with the feeling: "It always happens to me/why didn't you..."

In TA the importance of racket feelings is to detect when someone is in their Script. This doesn't mean they are bad, but it helps to understand how they continue to feel bad when there's no immediate reason for it. Or when someone reacts "from another time" to you.

In everyday life, the best thing is follow you own natural feelings and behave accordingly.

Bob Goulding's formula for dealing with feelings appeals to me.

1. What am I feeling? Name it.

2. What am I feeling bad about.

3. Is it about something past, present or future?

4. What can I do about it? List possibilities.

5. Whether I do something about it or not, will I be happy?

We have to let go of the guarantee that we are going to get what we want. We can feel good or bad. We can be happy or unhappy. Feeling good and happy is most likely if we stay in the here and now. We feel bad when things go wrong, then we do something or not, and in time feel good again. Unless you are determined to feel bad, then that's up to you.

TA teaches people to take responsibility for what they feel, and stop blaming the world, the past or others. Some people are never so happy as when they are miserable. It's hard to lay aside a racket, when it's "worked" for you all your life.

In a television film devoted to the life and work of Ronnie Laing, he describes a session working with depression.

"I remember one particular character who was absolutely suicidal, tremendously depressed, in the deepest depths of despair. And I asked him "What was the last time you remember being happy? Scan the last 24, 48 hours to when you last felt OK."

I got him into what he enjoyed. He would go out for a walk and whistle his favourite tune. So we got into this. At the end of 50 minutes we were exchanging jokes.

As he got to the door, he suddenly remembered he'd come to me because he was suicidal and he started to object that he hadn't got his money's worth. He hadn't spent his time going into his depression. I said, "You've had 50 minutes with me and you're not depressed now. Don't you think you might go away and think about what happened between us, that you've forgotten about your depression for a bit."

The best way to keep depressed is to keep thinking about your depression. You forget about it if you can. And if you can't, oh alright, we'll have to go into it!"

This illustrates graphically that people can be helped to switch out of feeling bad, by finding a source of good feelings. They don't need to go through all the rigmarole of discovering the cause of their depression or whatever. If they insist that they can't get out of it, I suggest that they spend the whole of the next week feeling bad! In doing so they have to make a conscious effort to stay in a bad place, and realise how they do it and the amount of energy they use. None of my clients have lasted more than two days. One reported breaking into uncontrollable laughter at her effort!

The place of feelings

I have seen TA as listed under cognitive therapies in some text books. This is understandable, as one of the aims of TA is to help people to think clearly, so that they can get the best out of their lives, and not be cluttered up with useless feelings or outdated rules.

However, I think that most TA therapists would regard the expression of feelings to be vitally important in the process of change. The more aware a person is of his feelings, the more likely it is that he will be creative, genuine and successful. It is my view that how a person deals with his feelings is not good or bad per se. While I encourage people to have feelings and support myself in what I feel, I do not hold with having feelings for the sake of it. Some people will never be or need to be expressive emotionally. It helps, however, if we validate our feelings and gain what Claude Steiner calls "emotional literacy".

When I am working with clients, I am constantly checking out how I feel.

Is it a racket? Something to do with me?

Is it a genuine response to what the client is doing?

Does it belong to me? or am I experiencing some feeling which the client is avoiding?

I do not hesitate to express my feelings if they fit what is happening - quite often I discover that what I am experiencing is the client's forbidden real feeling in response to his racket.

In the chapter on Changing, I shall deal with the place of emotions more fully. Sufficient to say here, that the therapeutic relationship in TA provides permission for people to experience their real feelings and to express what they feel in a safe environment.

EXERCISES

We are now going to go through a process to help you discover how you are with your feelings. First it is important for you to find out what is your main racket feeling.

Look back over the past week, month or year and check what kind of feelings you have most frequently. What's your favourite feeling? It's likely to be what you feel under the following circumstances:

When things go wrong

When you're alone

When you're under stress

When you're needy and doing nothing about it

When someone treats you badly

It hangs around for quite a while.

Often it has a quality which is affected by an attitude, e.g. miserable, helpless, useless, unworthy, paralysed, fussy, frustrated, defeated, niggly, worried, frenetic, hassled. It is quite possible that you will have more than one racket feeling, but most of us recognise an emotional state that is very familiar.

Now make a statement about you that fits this racket feeling, e.g. I am bound to fail. Now ask yourself how you got to be like that? Was this a feeling that was permitted at home?

What would happen if you decided to give up feeling like that?

Now let's look at a range of feelings and see how you experience them.

How are you on ANGER... FEAR... SADNESS... GLADNESS?

Which feelings do you have a lot of? which rarely or never?

Rate yourself on the following scale for each of the above feelings.

I express:

Anger..................OFTEN..............SOMETIMES....RARELY..........NEVER

Fear....................OFTEN..............SOMETIMES....RARELY..........NEVER

Sadness..............OFTEN..............SOMETIMES....RARELY..........NEVER

Gladness............OFTEN..............SOMETIMES....RARELY..........NEVER

Check on what you tell yourself about having or not having these feelings.

Do you feel a lot inside and do not show it? What's your objection?

Does it differ with some people or in different situations? List the differences. How do you explain them?

Imagine you are caught in a traffic jam. How do you usually feel?

> What's the matter with all these drivers?
>
> Why does this always happen to me?
>
> If I sit here for much longer I'll die
>
> People will never forgive me for being late
>
> It's all my fault, I should have left earlier.
>
> Might as well resign myself to it.
>
> or what?

Notice that the traffic does not make you feel bad.

What you feel belongs to you. You bring your own feelings into play in any situation. Someone else may experience quite a different feeling in the same circumstances.

Games

How to fail without really trying

We all want to get our own way. We may believe that other people won't give us what we want. So we have to trick them into it.

One way is by getting into a racket as we discussed previously. If this doesn't work or the strokes from the racket run out, we escalate into a game. Now we are playing a role. We are not aware of what we are doing. At the time we think that we mean what we are saying.

We use a coded message (*an ulterior transaction*), of which the hook has a bait (*con*): an attraction the other can't refuse. Otherwise he would say "Get lost!" The weakness or need (*gimmick*) of the other player causes him to "bite". The surprise ending comes when the ulterior message is de-coded (*switch*) and comes into awareness. Both players experience a moment of confusion (*Cross-up*). The pay-off is a familiar feeling (*racket*) for each of them.

Eric Berne devised this formula to show the elements of a game:

$$Con + Gimmick = Response - Switch - Crossup - Pay\text{-}off$$

Games in TA are a way of relating to people which proves what I believe about myself or others. The start of the game has a sense of "Maybe this time..." The end is familiar and goes like: "There you are...", "What did I tell you...", "You see...", "There I go again... ", "Why does this always happen to me?"

There is a hope that you will be able to resolve something in the past, but somehow (out of your awareness) the way you relate, or who you relate to, or the timing or the situation, conspire to end up bad for you *(the Pay-off)*.

Now the important thing about playing games is that it is done without Adult awareness, particularly of the consequences. If a person is aware of the emotional level of his transaction, he is manoeuvring the other person, not playing a game. Therefore, only in extreme cases of actual damage can we attach blame. But it is my experience that people will not stop playing games because they recognise - after the event - that it is bad for them and others, only when they see a better way of relating. The addiction to racket feelings is strong and long term.

Essentially, I see people playing games either because they do not wish to get close to people, but "pretend" to be interested, or because they want to be close but just do not know how - so the game is a failure to attach or be intimate. Intimacy involves people being straight and open with each other about their needs and feelings.

Some examples of popular games will give you a flavour of these familiar experiences:-

Look How Hard I've Tried
You start off putting a lot of energy often into something you don't really want to do, in order to get appreciated or rewarded. In some way you fail. The pay-off is useless suffering, being blameless or not getting any help.

Jeff decides to build a self-contained flat in his house to increase the family income because his wife has been made redundant. She wants to move, but he wants to stay put. He has a demanding job but works every spare moment. He doesn't ask for help but gets a lot of praise for his efforts, in spite of putting his back out. Secretly he's trying to get his wife's affection, but all she gives is sympathy out of guilt. Anyway he thinks: "You can't blame me if things don't work out. Look how hard I've tried!"

Uproar

Often played by couples who set out to discuss a problem. Lucy fixes up a holiday in the spring but Tom wants to postpone it to when he is not so busy. Lucy feels wronged and wants Tom to give in. Tom insists that if he goes, they will be short of money through lost business. "You're always doing this" says Lucy. "You've got no interest in my work" says Tom. And quickly the original issue gets lost. All sorts of complaints come out about their marriage and the stakes rise so high that the holiday becomes an excuse for all sorts of abuse and the grounds for separation. It ends in guilt and withdrawal, and the problem does not get solved.

Kick Me

In this game a person will be doing something apparently harmless or helpful, but will so infuriate the other in some way that he gets rejected. I remember a member of a group who came with a bag of sweets and handed them round at regular intervals. This seemed to be such a nice gesture that people went along with it, until, as one person was talking about a sensitive issue, there was this rustle of sweet papers. Whereupon nearly everyone got mad with him. He was so hurt, he never came back.

Rapo

The "con" or bait here is an ambiguous invitation which appears sexual. This can be a frivolous remark, a late night drink, and offer to stay the night, go away for the weekend or to sleep together. The response may involve some mutual flirting, but when the other person makes a sexual move, there is a strong rejection.

Now I've Got You, S.O.B.

Cynthia is on her honeymoon with George, when his mother calls saying she is ill and he must come back. So they return. Cynthia says nothing. Many times this pattern is repeated and she goes along with it. After ten years she sues

George for divorce, and hires a lawyer to take him "to the cleaners". George is bewildered with her vindictiveness. "Why are you doing this to me?" She replies: "Do you remember when you spoiled our honeymoon by putting your mother before me? I hated you for that. And now it's my turn to spoil things!"

At the end of this section there is a list of popular games with possible ways of dealing with people who "hook" you. Remember it takes two to play!

Every game is a drama played out of awareness with each person acting a role which excludes some relevant information.

The Drama Triangle

The Drama Triangle below has three different roles:-

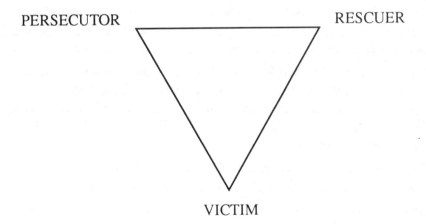

PERSECUTOR   RESCUER

VICTIM

In the *Victim* role a person believes he is helpless or worthless, incapable of knowing what is good for him, or how to take care of himself. He also believes that others are better than him, and have the power to do things for him which he cannot do for himself. So there are Victims looking for a Rescuer, and those looking for a Persecutor. Victims always transact from their negative Adapted Child ego state.

The *Persecutor* controls others from his negative Critical Parent by putting people down, blaming, being vindictive, punitive or destructive in order to keep others in the wrong. He persecutes those he considers to be bad, inferior or worthless. They need to be put in their place and told what to do and think.

In the *Rescuer* role people have a need to be needed. They subtly control others by being helpful without any real regard for the well-being of the other person. Rescuers are more concerned to feel important at the expense of exploiting the Victim. The purpose here is to make others dependent on the Rescuer, so that they will not be able to leave him.

The Drama Triangle shows clearly how players switch roles when the "game is up". The switch comes when either player reveals the previously hidden ulterior message, which results in the bad pay-off. The reason for the "drama" - the way people move - is that they are playing the game on two different levels, social and emotional. What game players *do* is different to what they *feel*.

I find it fascinating that while for instance one person may be rescuing at a social level (he looks helpful), underneath he may feel like a Victim. So his rescue is a ploy to finish up feeling bad. Victims on the other hand can feel vengeful for the position they're in, and find a way to collect enough bad feelings to blame the Rescuer for their plight.

Player A *rescues* to cover his feelings of inadequacy *(Victim)*.

Player B plays *Victim* to cover his feelings of revenge *(Persecutor)*.

Whatever roles people play socially, there is evidence that we have potentially all three roles Rescuer, Persecutor and Victim. Depending on the game one of the hidden roles will come to the surface and be acted out to end the game.

Here is an example of the game of "Why Don't You .. Yes, But..." which illustrates the moves in the Drama Triangle.

You play Victim (but feel blaming) till you've shown I'm no use and feel angry enough to persecute me. And I play Rescuer (but feel a Victim) and I stay in that role until I have collected enough bad feelings (frustration, failure etc.) to move to Victim.

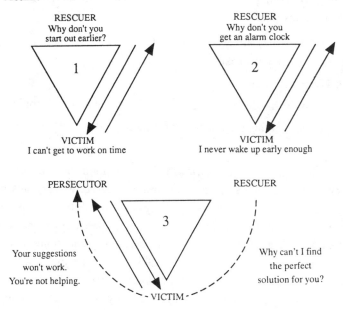

The conditions which are present in playing games:

One or both don't know what they want

They don't believe they can get what they want

They are scared or don't know how to ask for what they want.

Therefore they have to relate to others indirectly in code - ignoring *(discounting)* the most important aspect in the relationship or the situation. Both parties are temporarily happy because they are engaged, and getting strokes (albeit unwittingly)

People usually play games they learnt in childhood in order to maximise the flow of strokes - positive or negative. Consequently they believe in adult life that is the only way to do it. If they ask straight, they won't get what they want, whatever that is. Quite often people forget what they really want and go for what they can con the other person into giving them. Although the pay-offs of games is a bad feeling and confirms their belief about themselves or other people, there is usually a recurring pattern of behaviour which is intended to get their needs met. "Maybe this time..."

If games always finish up bad, why do people play them?

1. In order to get strokes

2. To structure time

3. To confirm a distorted view of themselves and other people

4. To avoid taking responsibility for their needs

5. To keep others around

Everyone plays games. How seriously depends upon the proportion of time spent against more satisfying activities, and the degree. Some games are played at a light socially acceptable level *(1st degree)* - like flirting at a party. Others are acted out in private *(2nd degree)* and the pay-offs are emotionally damaging and the effects can go on for long periods of time, sometimes years after. A game of Uproar can result in a partner walking out of the house (with or without the children or the money) leaving the other person devastated. I heard of a woman who took her children and all the money and left her husband in such a way. He spent the next two years in and out of court to restore contact with his children and some share of the family resources. In this case the game moved from Uproar to Courtroom. He gave up working to defend himself. She had a nervous breakdown as a result of his vengeful pursuit.

When games are played for keeps *(3rd degree)* they result in permanent physical harm. The example above was dangerous but no-one ended up in a hospital, prison or the mortuary.

Ten rules for keeping out of games

The useful thing about understanding games is that when you become aware of regularly feeling bad about an encounter, you can begin to see what happened and *how* you got into it in the first place. Then you can begin to change the way you initiate or respond to others by being straight. This list is illustrated by the game of Uproar as described on page 52.

1. Make sure you have a good supply of positive strokes.

Uproar players are guilt-mongers. So they need strokes for being straight, pleasing themselves as well as others, and finding people who can accept their anger.

2. Confront the first "come-on" (see chart on p59)

Avoid getting into fights with no rules. Don't let your guilt push you into trying to make things right.

3. Notice the bad feeling and what you are telling yourself and don't buy the bad pay-off.

As soon as you start feeling angry, stop and make a contract to keep to the subject, set a time limit. If you're feeling low, postpone discussion.

4. Look for another pay-off which values your senses of OK-ness.

Uproar games players need to feel separate and need permission to be apart.

5. Lower the level/degree. Keep it light. "Whoops! there we go again."

Take a break. Get into mutual complaining about how awful things are!

6. Don't make things worse by escalating into another game or level where the stakes are higher.

Keep to the holiday. Don't insist on being right. Agree as much as possible. Don't shout. Don't hit low.

7. Ask yourself: "What am I really doing with you?"

I know I am asking you to postpone the holiday, but I am really trying to get my way and keep control of you (The extreme could be - I want you to worship at the shrine of my decisions/mistakes!!) Give it up.

8. Look for the line or action which gets you going.

It may be very simple like "By the way ..." or your partner's rigid posture or facial expression.

9. What is the secret message?

   "You always let me down" "You never take an interest in me"

10. Don't do things with others you don't want to do.

   e.g. getting into rows, talking late at night, going on going on. This keeps your guard up. Check what you're *doing*. Not what you're *hoping* to gain or avoid - usually out of reach in games.

GAMES PEOPLE PLAY - See Game Chart on next page

ROLE SWITCH of starting player in Drama Triangle

COME-ON - 1st move which involves a discount

PAYOFF - Racket feeling or Mythical belief.

Generally the way out of playing games is to be aware of your interest, take responsibility for what you are doing, don't blame others, stay in the here and now, give positive strokes and only transact from positive Nurturing Parent, Adult or Free Child.

GAMES PEOPLE PLAY

GAME	ROLE Switch	COME-ON Invitation	PAYOFF	CONFRONTATION to avoid playing game
Why Don't You ...Yes But	V → P	I've got a problem	Justifiable anger	Thats a difficult problem What are you going to do? Don't give advice
I'm Only Trying To Help You	R → V	You only have to ask me	Frustration	Thanks for the offer. I'll tell you what I want
Do Me Something	V → P	You're so good at this	Proving problems can't be solved	I'm not much good at that What could you do?
What Would You Do Without Me	R → P	You can rely on me for anything	Showing others to be incapable	I'd like to make my own mistakes
Kick Me	R/P→V	How can you kick me when I'm so ...	Rejection	You're asking for it but - How about a hug?
Stupid	V → P	You're right. I'm dim.	You're not so clever	Don't laugh.Change subject
Peasant	V → P	Tell me. You're the boss	Inadequate	What if I don't tell you?
Wooden Leg	V → P	What can you expect of me	Opting out	It seems hopeless
Poor Me	V → P	I'm just not good enough	Enjoying misery	You must feel bad
Harried	R → V	I can cope with anything	Collapse	There's always something to be done. You can go at your own pace
Look How Hard I've Tried	R → P	Hard work & suffering	Blameless	Its a hard life. Don't pressure
Blemish	P → V	Thats alright but ...	Avoiding own problem	Don't give me all that crap. I know my faults
Uproar	P → V	I want to be with you Lets talk about this	Angry withdrawal - silent or noisy	Time out. Agree to leave it & come back later when things have cooled down
Rapo	V → P	I'm available	You're no good	What's your interest in me? I like you but I don't want sex.
See What You Made Me Do	V → P	I'm more interested in you than what I'm doing	Making others guilty	Its all my fault, huh? Leave me out of this.
If It Weren't For You	P → V	Why do you always stop me from doing what I want?	Avoiding the fear of doing it anyway	Who Me? What are you scared of?
Now I've Got You, You S.O.B.	V → P	I'll have to go along with you	Being one-up Getting even	What the price? You've got me. I give up.

CHAPTER THREE

HOW THE STORY BEGAN

Lifescripts

Once upon a time... when we were very young, too young to think for ourselves, too dependent to change the circumstances, and too small to know better, we were faced with big people usually parents, who looked after us in certain ways and told us what to do and how to be - some good, some not so good for us.

We figured out with our Little Professor (the instructor part of our child ego state) the best way for us to get through that experience. Depending on what kind of people they were, our parents gave us messages about ourselves and others, some helpful, some unhelpful or destructive. We didn't know any better then, so we believed them whether we liked it or not. So we adapted to suit or frustrate them.

And so we begin to write our script - the story of our life. By the age of five the basic outline has been written. Then it had to be rehearsed and refined at stages in our development until adolescence when it was ready to be performed with other people to act out the parts.

Based on that early experience we made certain decisions about ourselves and other people, which we have made into a pattern for life.

EXERCISE

Write the outline of a play or a film (make it as long or as short as you like - most people find that 500 words is about right) that would fit the story of your life. Invent a character like you and tell your story in the third person.

This can help you to recognise the general pattern in your drama, the chief actors, the main plot and sub-plots, the recurring theme(s) and the way you have played your part in it. This will be useful for you to refer to as you work through this chapter so that you can check how the elements of lifescripts fit your story.

Script themes

A handy way of recognising your life drama is to give it a title which has a theme. Here's a few examples:

Being helpful	Saving for a rainy day
Waiting for him/her	Living it up
Going on, going on	Saving the world
Holding on	Playing second fiddle
Missing the boat	Being good.
Living from crisis to crisis	Wasting time
Not really here	Always left out
Sorry	Playing the fool
I did it my way	Taking risks
Keep moving	Falling in love
Not enough time	Frightened to death
Being liked	Indispensable
The life and soul of the party	Playing hard to get
Being used	Throwing it away

What is your script theme?

Give a title to the story of your life.

The setting

Once upon a time ... there was a little baby which was you. You were born into a family in a certain country with certain rules which kept you safe but at the same time imposed restraints on the family you grew up in.

What were the rules of life in the culture/country of your birth/upbringing?

What kind of lives did your grandparents lead?

What did your parents inherit from their own background? My father knew little of his family, due to the fact that his father was disabled at the age of 40 and he and his sister were sent away to boarding school, and but for the generosity of my grandmother's family might have landed up in the workhouse.

Your family inherited a tradition which affected much of what your parents did. Unwittingly they passed on much of what they had learned from their upbringing. This was both a blessing and a curse. You were not to know till later which. For a long time children accept the norms of their family without question. It's the only one they know. It wasn't until the age of six when I went away to live with my godparents at the beginning of the war that I realised how different my family was. I remember crying every time I had to leave them. Life at home seemed empty compared to the rich life of growing up on their farm.

What was going on in your family before you were born? My parents were just recovering from the effects of the Depression. My father was working in London, living in digs, driving back to my mother and sister in Manchester every weekend, until he could find a place for them all to live. Times were hard, when I was conceived. This pre-birth period is regarded by some (in Primal work) as vital in setting the pattern for our lives. That unconscious formation is part of a person's script.

How do you imagine you were greeted at birth? Were you welcome? Unexpected? A burden? Difficult? Unwanted? Were you the right sex? Did you save your parents' marriage? Bring them together? Push them apart?

What was the story of your birth?

What do you imagine they said when you were born?

What was your position in the family?

What was your favourite story and who are you in it?

How was your name chosen?

What did they call you as a child?

Are you glad you were born?

What is your earliest memory?

SURVIVAL KITS - We are not helpless victims of our parents

For the first few months and years you had little or no control over these influences on your life. Even now they are so strong that they still affect your life and choices. But somehow you got through in your own way.

You knew from the beginning what felt good and bad for you, but you were too small to change the setting of your birth. You couldn't pack your bags and go and find another family. So you had to accept what was given.

However, even at the earliest age you knew that you could do something about it. You could let on with sounds which mostly got a better response. You cried and got held. You smiled and were praised. But you learned that you couldn't get some things, for example, you cried and didn't get held. And some things weren't allowed so you adapted. That kept you safe. You gave up something. But you had to survive and get your needs met in the best way you knew how. You learnt how to get as much stroking as you could.

The fact is that in spite of either ideal parenting or appalling abuse, people seem to use these experiences for or against themselves in some way independently of the conditions of their childhood.

Some of my clients have been through years of living with parents who constantly assaulted them, and although this has had some detrimental effects, they have come through remarkably well. They have become loving parents, successful or creative in their lives. Others seem to have been well cared for by parents who were interested in them, and yet run themselves into hurtful relationships or lacked purpose in life. It seems there is not always a clear direct connection with conditions in which they grew up. I believe that we all have a secret self which says "No matter what you do to me, you'll never get me". Some describe this as the spiritual part or the instinct for life. However, the treatment we got does not necessarily predict the outcome. Whatever messages our parents gave us, we made our own unique response.

In my experience, both personally and professionally, people constantly surprise me how they got through some terrible ordeals. True, they are affected by their early traumas, and some do not recover well, but we are not the victims of our parents. Whatever they said or did, the child has the power to accept or reject their messages.

So, lifescripts are written by us in order to **survive**. The way each of us got through indicates our individual power within the situation to choose.

How did *you* survive?

Some children rebel, some conform; some keep quiet, some have tantrums; some go crazy, some stop eating, some say to themselves "I'll show you".

Nicky was a bright lad, but his father was an alcoholic who had fits of rage, constantly shouted at him and hit him; told him he was stupid and would never amount to anything. Nick grew up in constant fear, but secretly said to himself "I'll show you!" He lived in a dream world. And that is how he survived. He failed at everything, but he never gave up. Eventually, through sheer hard work and determination, he got to college and became a successful doctor. He made two decisions which got him through. One was to be a good man to show his father to be bad. The other was to work hard, even if it killed him, to prove his father to be wrong. He succeeded. That's how he survived a miserable childhood. It was much later after a breakdown, that he learned it was O.K. to get angry and gave up "working himself to death".

Life positions

As time went by, you were treated in certain ways - the way you were touched, held, looked at, talked to "You're wonderful" or "You're naughty...", "That's good" or "Be quiet", from which you decided whether you were OK or not. Depending on what you made of the way your parents behaved towards you, one another and others in and around the family, you also formed a view of the world - which left you with a number of possible decisions:-

It's a good world, someday I'll make it better

It's a bad world, someday I'll get my own back by doing something bad

It's a mediocre world, where I do what I have to do and have fun in between

A tough world which I have to put up with or resist

A hard world where I bend or struggle to keep going or a dreary world where I sit around hoping or a futile world, where I give up.

Although these can be changed in later life, for some people these remain fixed, and a plan is devised to last for life.

If that's the way things are, and this is who I am ... then this is how I'm going to live.

It is an unsolved puzzle as to why, on the basis of similar experience, children make widely differing decisions. There are some theories which assert that the genetic make-up of each baby is far more powerful than the effect of parenting. I do not share this view, although it explains a lot of contradictory behaviour and the idea of genetic memory going back generations is fascinating. I prefer to see that every conception is unique and that in some way we have a secret self which sorts out in its own way how to live. Also, parents are changing all the time in their ways of parenting. Some actually improve and become more relaxed in parenting their offsprings and there is much less fear around.

Causes of scripting

Why do we as children make decisions, write a life story and then make choices which can be so limiting or destructive?

They are not made rationally, but based on intuitive feelings and sensations, when *safety* is the primary concern. Satisfaction and pleasure are secondary.

We needed the protection of our parents so if that was threatened we would do anything to keep safe. We hadn't got the power or knowledge to take any course of action which might be better. We chose to be a certain way because within the limits of the family setting anything else would or could be worse: "This may not be good but it's not as bad as ..."

So the implications of parental message are "Do what I say, please me, don't do that, and you will be safe." "You may be uncomfortable, but that's for your own good." "That's what you're supposed to do or else..."

All script messages constrict the Free Child and cause him to distrust his own wishes and experience.

We needed to be loved, so we tried all sorts of ways to get it, or the next best thing, being admired. You may have figured out: "If I am not loved then it's because I'm bad". Or you may (at a later stage) have decided that they are not good enough and reject them, and then hopefully or despairingly go off to find someone who is good enough.

When we grow up it's too late to get back all that we "should" have got. But when things go wrong we may re-visit that magical world and believe that some day my prince/princess will come. Eric Berne said that the most important decision was to give up hoping that Santa Claus will come. A lot of people are unhappy because they are "waiting for Santa Claus" to save them, solve their problems or grant their wishes. If only I do this or that then perhaps my ship will come in.

What are you waiting for?

How messages are passed on - Transmission
In addition to the way you were treated, your parents conveyed messages about you directly or indirectly by the way they behaved. You may have received the message in a different way from what they intended. You learned how to be you and how to behave from them:

Telling you what you are

You're a bad boy!	You're just like your mother
You're always in the way	Such a helpful little lad
You're a handful	Everyone says you're going places

Showing you how

Mother sulks when father criticises her but says nothing

Father works hard and is always tired.

Mother and Father give each other a hug when things go wrong

Suggesting what you should do, think or feel

Don't bother me!   What's the problem, son?

Mother overburdened   Mother always dresses well

Father never there   Father is always on time.

Now it is unlikely that a message will have a lifelong impact on a child, unless one or more of the following factors are present in the delivery:

Trauma

A dramatic event (particularly when very small) such as a road accident, or being taken away from mother or having some crippling illness. The messages drawn from such experiences are either pre- or non-verbal.

Repetition

Telling a child he is silly occasionally is not going to have much effect, but "You're a stupid boy" repeated over and over whenever he gets something wrong is likely to stick with him unless he discovers later that clever people make mistakes, or proves he's not stupid.

Intensity

Verbal messages can be delivered with such power (in rage, fear or despair) that children will feel put down and believe awful things will happen, if they are not careful. Non-verbal messages can carry even more powerful impact such as locking children up, hitting, abusing sexually or any severe punishments.

All these are negative strokes and as such convey more power than positive strokes. Therefore negative messages are more likely to be followed when there is little positive re-enforcement.

Source (which parent carries most power?)

Then again it depends which parent is seen as more powerful. For example, if a mother dresses her daughter attractively, and says "You're lovely", that could be more dominant than father's sexual put downs, because mother carries the strongest sexual power in the marriage. At the same time it could be very confusing.

Little children see the world in a dramatic, magical way and deduce all sorts of strange things.

If mother is ill, it's my fault

If father goes away, he didn't love me

If I don't do something, all sorts of terrible things might happen.

I wished there'd be a war, and the next day war was declared.

In our dreams and fantasies we re-live that primitive haunted, mythical world.

FANTASY EXERCISE

The following fantasy exercise will put some flesh onto the bones of your script.

Go back to when you were about six or seven.

What was it like for you up to this age?

See the place you lived. Who was living there?

Go out of your home and look at it.

What sort of feelings do you have?

Now I want you to imagine you are going to school.

See the way you went. How you got there. Who did you meet?

Spend a bit of time recalling what happened on a typical day.

Now school is over, and you are going home.

Experience the sights and sounds as you return.

Go inside your home. Who's there?

Look around and find your **mother** (if she was there; if not, a mother figure).

Where is she? What is she doing?

Now get her attention.

See the expression on her face?

*What is the one thing she says you must do at all costs?...	PRESCRIPTION
*Whatever happens, the one thing you must not do is ...	INJUNCTION
*What did she want you to be?...	PROGRAMME

Leave your mother and find your father (if he was there; if not, a father figure).

Where is he? What is he doing?

Get his attention. How does he look at you?

*What is it he tells you you must make sure to do? ...	PRESCRIPTION
*What is it that you must make sure you don't do? ...	INJUNCTION
*What did he want you to be? ...	PROGRAMME

From the answers to the marked * questions, you can recognise the messages they gave you. Fill them in on the chart below, using the example as a guide.

Notice the relationship between them - how one supports or contradicts another.

SCRIPT MATRIX

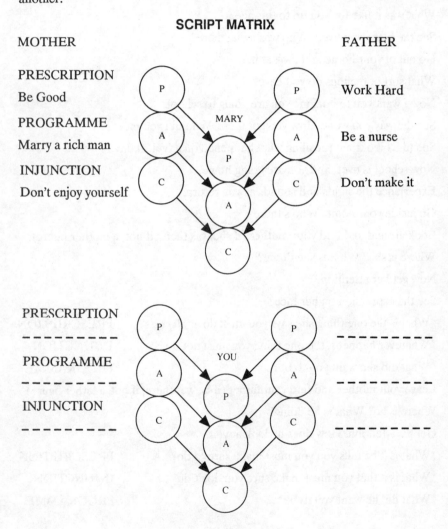

MOTHER

PRESCRIPTION
Be Good

PROGRAMME
Marry a rich man

INJUNCTION
Don't enjoy yourself

FATHER

Work Hard

Be a nurse

Don't make it

MARY

PRESCRIPTION
- - - - - - - -

PROGRAMME
- - - - - - - -

INJUNCTION
- - - - - - - -

YOU

- - - - - - - - -

- - - - - - - - -

- - - - - - - - -

Elements in your lifescript

On the basis of this, see if you can figure out your major life decisions - one that is still with you.

Rule of thumb: **The parent of the opposite sex tells you what to do and the parent of the same sex shows you how to do it.**

The prescription *(or counterscript)* determines your style of life and comes from nurturing parent slogans, and only become meaningful in later childhood and adolescence, for example: Work hard, Be Good.

When these well-intentioned messages are felt to be compulsive, we call them *drivers* - they push you into script. Thus they play a significant part in "keeping the story going" (see Chapter Four).

You have been given a *programme* for life (nursing, marriage) - the means of fulfilling your script. If not, you'll find another way to carry out your script decision.

The script injunctions control your ultimate destiny. These messages come from the scared Child of a critical parent and take effect early in life (by two or three) e.g. Don't make it. Don't enjoy yourself.

If these are in *harmony*, then they may not be noticed. The script messages are complementary. In the example above, Mary may decide to be a nurse, work double shifts which will keep her out of trouble (Be good). In the meantime, she will be hoping to meet a rich man who will release her from her struggle to be good. Either she won't make it, or she won't enjoy life, and that will be her script decision.

If they are in *conflict*, they may bring chaos, and the script injunction will win. Examples:

AND / OR	
Prescription	**Injunction**
Be a lady	Don't trust men.
Make money	Don't be close
Look good	Drop dead

As long as you are a lady, work hard or look good, you won't drop dead or feel lonely. This then becomes a limited insurance against the awful things that might happen if you don't go on with the prescription. Also in the hierarchy of Injunctions some are more damaging than others so we may settle for one which may not be so bad to live with, like: Don't feel, rather than: Don't exist.

In the previous chapter we have already seen how we "tell our story", in the way we relate to others and experience feelings. So we can now recognise how our predictable feelings (*rackets*) and behaviour (*games*) are a re-enactment of our early script decision, and limit the way we exchange strokes. They all fit into the picture of life we created long ago, in order to get through.

However, not all our life is scripted. There is a mixture of givens and what we choose. We are all born with the potential for creativity, spontaneity, and intimacy. We have been given our inheritance, our family, genetics, luck, our natural abilities, mental and physical. On the basis of these we make our early intuitive decisions. Later on we make choices about how we are going to live based on our understanding of ourselves and the world. Into this mix there are coincidences and external events outside of our control. We use our energy in a certain way and make an effort to make something out of all this. With insight and effort we can make new decisions based on free choices. For this we need to gain new permissions to do what was prohibited by our parents.

Injunctions and permissions

An *injunction* is an implicit message given by parents, usually non-verbally, and often unconsciously. In childhood we respond to these with a decision. There are twelve injunctions (Bob and Mary Goulding) with the corresponding permissions needed for growth. Injunctions are prohibitions, permissions allow freedom to choose:

Injunctions	Permissions
Don't Be	You can be alive
Don't Be You	You can be yourself, who you are, the sex you are, the race
Don't Be a Child	You can have fun
Don't Grow Up	You can be your age, make your own life
Don't Make It	You can make it, be successful
Don't Be Important	You can have needs and ask for what you want
Don't Belong	You can stay around, and belong in the way that suits you
Don't Be Close	You can be physically and emotionally close to others
Don't Be Well (or Sane)	You can be healthy and still get strokes
Don't Think	You can think clearly for yourself and solve problems
Don't Feel	You can have your sensations and emotions
Don't (do anything)	You can take risks and be safe

Although we may not have got the permissions we needed when young, we can gain these later in life in a variety of ways - watching other people, being treated by others differently from our parents - we can take on board new messages from others we respect - teachers, clergy, youth leaders, aunts and uncles, friends, partners, and also therapists! In the final chapter on Changing the Story, I will describe the methods I use to help people to change their early script decisions and gain new permissions to counter the negative messages from their childhood.

The second part of this chapter is aimed at showing the various patterns in adult life that have been derived from early childhood and written by us to form our script.

Scripts in adult life

By now I hope you have begun to recognise something of your life pattern, and how the foundation for your later decisions has been laid down long ago. You learnt how to deal with your worst fears by writing your script.

Later in adult life these early decisions and messages continue, in spite of the fact that they are out of date. Although we now have more information, and can see what they are, changing is another matter. As St. Paul said: "The good that I would I cannot do and the evil that I would not that I do".

Now we will see how these early strategies are acted out in the present when things go wrong, like they did when we were young. Something in the present presses a button and sets us off into script. When this happens we react in the same way as we did in childhood when we were faced with a similar situation. We see the world in the same way as we perceived it when we were small.

What sets it off? Why do we keep repeating the same familiar behaviour or feelings? The answers to these questions are particular to each person but there are some common triggers, like when something stressful occurs or when you are faced with something difficult or unexpected, when someone treats you badly, you spend too much time alone, people begin to crowd you, you fail, someone leaves you, you are faced with an important decision, when you are stroke starved, and so on. These are conditions which can take you back to old patterns.

Moving into script means you distort external reality and return to some old scene and repeat it by thinking and behaving in the same way that you did in the early painful experience. You are usually not aware of the old scene because the stimulus in the present is so strongly reminiscent that you believe your present perception is "real". It is as though we are connected to a great rubber band which hooks us off into the past.

This experience is called "transference" in analytical psychology, and is used in analytical therapy to help the client to access archaic material. This projection can happen of course, whenever a person goes into any kind of therapy. For the client, the therapist can become anyone in the past (or the present) or, as often happens, the ideal person. In TA, we aim to use this process by making the client aware of it - by confronting the client with present reality.

DIAGRAM TO SHOW HOW WE RE-ENACT THE OLD PATTERN

in similar situations in the present

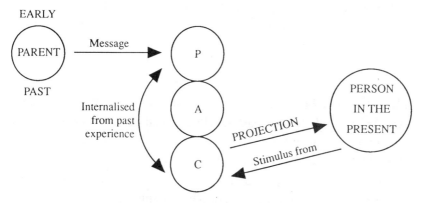

Imagines this is the same as in the past
feels and acts as before

And so when we are faced with certain problems which were painful in the past, we become like the child we were, unable to deal with them, and so resort to the self defeating ways we used then to get through.

Our script is that part of our personality which goes into automatic pilot (with very little thinking) every time we are faced with a person or situation that reminds us of the past. At best it restricts our freedom to respond. At worst it can drive us to feel or be destructive.

Another way of looking at this time warp is that we have a movie projector locked away in the back of our minds that has an activated memory switch which gets turned on under stress, and then we start playing "old movies" and projecting them on the present situation or person.

DIAGRAM OF PROJECTED IMAGE

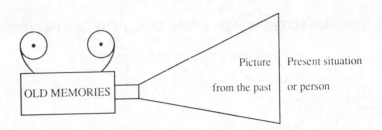

Think of a person/situation with which you always seem to finish up in a bad place. Ask yourself: "Who or what does that remind me of?" Then see what the similarity is between the two, and how you are projecting onto the present some past experience which is causing you so much difficulty.

Now look again at the person(s) or scene and write down what actually happened and notice how you could deal with it differently.

Notice how you make others fit your story. If they don't, how you look around to find others who will. We do this by playing games. This is how you tell the story. Why does this always happen to me? You confirm what you already believe - and nothing (least of all you) changes, though you may go on hoping that one day it will. You tell yourself:

"You can't trust anyone", but go on trusting people in an unrealistic way, and feel *frightened* of being alone.

"I can't depend on myself", so I go on living *unhappily* the way other people prescribe.

"Other people depend on me to look after them", so I don't get much for myself, feel deprived, unworthy, resentful but don't express *anger*.

Without realising it, we cling to the magical solutions of childhood and in repeating them, hold on to the belief that this is the way to avoid catastrophic expectations. Even when it looks as though I could be happy by doing something else, I fear it will all go wrong (The devil you know). It's hard to let go of my cherished beliefs. "I can't be happy unless... and strive vainly for some magical solution. "If only ..."

A little boy lived in constant fear of his father, who was a violent man. His way of coping was to be good and so avoid the terrible punishments he believed his father would carry out. Today he is a social worker but suffers from panic attacks whenever his clients complain. So he works harder to keep them happy.

CHOICES we make in adult life based on DECISIONS in childhood

There are a number of issues we face as adults which affect the way we live and feel about ourselves. We can draw a line between the choices we make and check whether they are made freely or in the belief that there is no other way, that's the way we are, based on childhood decisions. Then it will be worthwhile to review them and see if you want to change the balance.

Look at the following list and put a tick at the point between each of the two possibilities where you place yourself in the way you live and relate to others.

Love (Accepting) ....Power (Controlling)

Enjoying yourself ....Looking after others

Thinking ....Feeling

Belonging ....Being a Loner

Live now, pay later ....After .. I'll have fun

Going on ....Giving up

Success ....Intimacy

Doing ....Being

Taking risks ....Fear of Failure

Grow up ....Be a child

Think for yourself ....Let others do the thinking

Be yourself ....Please others

Perhaps, there are other issues which you are aware of. In which case, add them to the list. Now check the point you have ticked. Is this an Adult choice or an outdated decision? If you are aware of a need to change, put an arrow facing left or right to indicate the direction of change. This kind of review lies at the core of my work, for it shows that nothing is fixed in the past. With the right kind of permission, you can change almost anything. You may not want to. That's OK too. A permission is like a fishing permit. Just because you possess one, you haven't *got* to go fishing. But if you want to, you can!

Areas of scripting

Now let's take a look at a number of large areas of life where people are lacking important permissions. Their ability to function well is restricted, not through lack of ability or uncontrollable forces, but by self-limiting attitudes or behaviour dictated by early parental injunctions. This may be expressed (out of awareness) in various ways, like: I'll never be happily married. I don't have enough time to have a holiday. No-one cares about me. Life is a constant struggle. Everything is against me.

Now it's important to recognise the painful feelings behind these statements. At the same time to identify the parental message which is not true or accurate.

Below, under each heading, you will see the likely parent messages (injunctions) and beliefs which cause a blockage in that area of life. This is followed by the permission that is necessary for change, and an affirmation which will support you in breaking through the impasse of the early decision.

Sex

Messages: Don't be close. Don't feel

Beliefs: Sex is dirty, People who enjoy it aren't nice.

Permissions: You can enjoy your body. Expressing your sexual feelings is fine.

78

Education
Messages: Don't succeed. Don't think.

Beliefs: You're stupid. Those who don't have a proper education don't count.

Permissions: You can think for yourself. You can learn what you want to learn and use it.

Work
Messages: Don't make it. Don't be important. Don't enjoy life.

Beliefs: Be happy with what you've got. Life is a struggle.

Permissions: You can choose what is fulfilling for you. It's OK to enjoy your life. Take a break.

Health
Messages: Don't be well. Don't exist.

Beliefs: When you are well, no-one bothers. It's a crazy world.

Permissions: You are able to take care of yourself. Ask others for help.

Food
Messages: Don't feel your sensations. Don't be close. Don't grow up.

Beliefs: Eat what's put before you. Nobody loves you as you are.

Permissions: Eat what's good for you. You can choose how to be you.

Enjoyment
Messages: Don't feel good. Don't be a child.

Beliefs: Pleasure is a sign of weakness. Only kids can have fun.

Permissions: Responsible people can enjoy themselves. Have fun whenever you want.

Appearance

Messages:	Don't be important. Don't show off. Don't be attractive.
Beliefs:	Looking good is nothing but vanity. It's virtuous to be unattractive.
Permissions:	Chase the blues - buy some shoes! Being attractive feels good.

Friendship

Messages:	Don't be close, Don't be needy.
Beliefs:	You can't trust people. People will reject you, let you down.
Permissions:	You can let people be important to you. You can trust yourself with others. It's OK to ask.

Family

Messages:	Don't belong. Don't be you. Don't grow up.
Beliefs:	You've got to keep moving. Conforming is a trap. No-one is good enough for me.
Permissions:	You can be at home in a way that suits you. You can come and go and belong how you want.

Look at the above list and notice where you have a prohibiting injunction.

It is important to recognise that in each area of life we can be in script, or script-free. Quite often two or more areas are linked.

In order to function well, we need to have satisfying experiences and a reasonable amount of autonomy in at least half of these areas of scripting.

On the Pie Chart on the next page you will see a sample profile. Draw your own to indicate where you are in your life. Shaded areas indicate script. The clear areas are script-free.

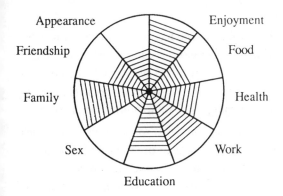

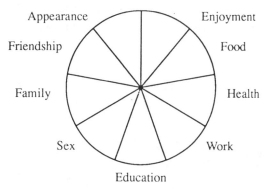

What is distinctive about the concept of scripts is that the way we live our lives is not accidental. We wrote it based on the perception of what we made of what was going on in childhood. We are not just victims of parental and environmental influences. In adult life we are not immediately aware of our early decisions, but as we get older, we begin to have a sense of a repetitive pattern, which we maintain by distorting reality, because we still believe our well-being is dependent on keeping going. Chapter Four will show the mechanism we use to do this.

Personally, I do not have much interest in emotional archaeology, digging up the past for the sake of it. We cannot change the past so what can we do? Understand it, relive it, stay in it, be bound by it, be free of it, forget it?

WHAT IS TA?

What I most value about TA is that Eric Berne has put his finger on how we experience in the present what happened or more accurately, what we thought happened, and found a language and system called script analysis to help us discover the origins of the patterns in our life. So all the clues are in the present and a therapist is a good detective helping his client to unravel the mystery.

By understanding your script, you can discover what you are doing now which is uncomfortable and blocking and decide what to do, think or feel about it. There are no musts. Each person can and does choose what to do about his past. People get on with their lives one way or another without radical change, and only go for help when either their script has run out or is causing them to be damaged or to be seriously dysfunctional.

Chapter Four

KEEPING THE STORY GOING

Once we have written the story of our life, we then maintain it by various means and devices. We have already seen in Chapter Two how we tell our story in the way we structure/use our time and relationships. In fact, we can trace in all the components of our personality and behaviour, elements of our script. (See the chart at the end of the book)

In this chapter you can discover how you keep your lifescripts going in the present and, how, by preventing the possibility of using certain parts of yourself, you limit your options for change.

FRAME OF REFERENCE

In the past we had to exclude certain reality which was painful or potentially harmful in order to keep safe. So we invented the world, including ourselves, to make sure that we could live as best as possible. Unfortunately, at the same time we excluded many aspects of life that could help us: parts of ourselves, possible experiences, and ways of relating. This expression of ourselves and our experience is called a *frame of reference*. It is the way in which we structure our responses from our ego states working together in a certain way which defines reality.

Gill's father died when she was very young, so she glamorises men from a distance. She believes that if she gets close to them, they will leave her. Her frame of reference doesn't allow her to trust men, unless she makes herself indispensable.

James was adopted and grew up with parents who had to struggle to make ends meet. He was bright but no-one showed any interest in him. So he decided to apply himself to making money. He now lives alone in a big house and feels a failure. Being a success is outside his frame of reference.

Jacqui Schiff and others were responsible for developing the material in this section as a result of their work with schizophrenics at the Cathexis Institute in California.

The frame of reference in each of us is the way our experience acts as a filter on reality. We are largely unaware of this. We have taken it for granted all our lives. It is derived from our early parenting which we have constructed to include what we believe and to exclude what we don't believe.

We only notice its existence when we come into conflict with others' frame of reference, or when it is painfully clear that what we are holding onto is against the evidence. So we have to extend the use of our senses and see, hear or feel more or change our understanding.

We all have to a greater or lesser extent a frame of reference which is a self-limiting way we regard ourselves and the world. To some extent this keeps us comfortable, but at the same time it maintains a view of life, which keeps us from solving problems and taking responsibility for ourselves.

Whenever something falls outside our frame of reference we discount it. It may be a feeling, a possibility, anything which might disturb the carefully constructed view we have of ourselves, others or the world generally. Your frame of reference is how you experience life, selecting some things and leaving out others. For example, some people are aware of nature, while others hardly notice the noise of the city; some people are sensitive to feelings, others have no sense of their own worth.

Frame of Reference

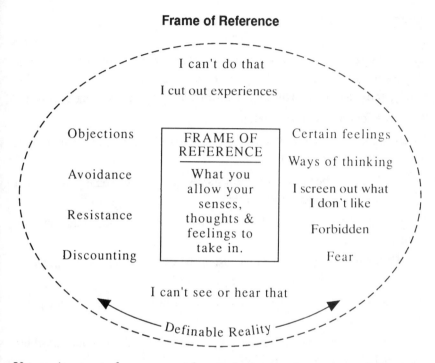

You can't get out of your present frame of reference, but you can change it by being aware of discomfort in your Child, (like: working all the time is no fun!) by taking in some new parenting from others. e.g. asking "How's it you can do that?"

At a simplistic level, if you increase your awareness, you can re-frame your attitudes or beliefs, so as to extend you frame of reference. A person who can't stand being alone doesn't have the same problem as someone who can't stand people. It all depends on which way you look at it!

The mechanism that we use to maintain our frame of reference and keep our script going is called *discounting*.

Discounting is a way of thinking which eliminates or distorts anything outside our frame of reference.

DISCOUNTING

Discounting is an internal process and cannot therefore be observed. It involves a distortion of a person's perception of himself, other people or definable reality, and is a selective ignoring of information related to solving a problem.

There are four levels of discounting.

Discounting the *existence* of something, denying that it is a problem, or that anything can be done about it.

> Fred, a member of a group, constantly arrives late. Some people don't notice and it doesn't bother others

Discounting the *significance* of it, ignoring the problem, not doing anything about it.

> One person notices Fred's persistent lateness, but he doesn't think it's important. "It's not worth bothering about".

Discounting the *possibility of changing it*, not solving the problem, doubting that any action is viable.

> Another person not only notices it, feels upset but doesn't think anything can be done. "People are always late".

Discounting a *person's ability to react differently*, to solve problems, or to act on options.

> A number of people sit quietly every week, saying to themselves: "I wish Eric would tell Fred to stop disrupting the group and come on time".

No discounting

> Finally one person says: "I'm really fed-up with you coming late every week. Will you please make an effort to get here on time?"

You can see from this example that when a problem remains unsolved, some aspect, information or possible action is being left out. Run this process through any situation or problem you have experienced and notice the level of discounting in yourself or others involved.

Discounting is a hidden process going on inside a person whenever he comes across some problem, situation, person or behaviour that he believes he cannot deal with. It is like an internal defence system that switches into automatic alert whenever "danger" threatens. That is how I cope with that, this is the only way I know to think or feel about that.

The effect of this is that we remain "passive" in dealing with our needs, people, situations, and expect someone else to do something for us without telling him.

We can only detect discounting therefore, by certain behaviours. We have already discussed the way people play games in order to avoid taking responsibility for themselves. The first transaction in a game always implies a discount. We can recognise this as a "passive" invitation for a game to be played. Now we will look at a cluster of other actions which can help us to be aware of how we keep "stuck" in our script and give us some clues about how we can get out of the rut.

PASSIVITY

Passivity is not necessarily a lack of activity. We experience it when something is not being said or done, we feel a "gap", a vacuum that is not being filled. It's like an unfinished sentence. When a person is passive in relation to a need, it always implies that someone else is supposed to know what it is and do something about it. Passivity can be encapsulated in that myth "If you love me, you will know what I want".

Passivity is the way we maintain our frame of reference and discount options for solving problems. There are four passive behaviours which are displayed in situations where a person either refuses to respond to external events, think about alternative action in order to achieve an objective or solve problems. They represent ways of initiating games in which we try to get other people to take responsibility for us and maintain over-dependent relationships.

Passive behaviours are learned through experiences in childhood when there was inadequate recognition given to a child's needs by his parents. They discounted him by responding to their own world of feelings and thoughts, instead of the actual reality of what was happening to him.

Doing nothing is using your energy to stop you from responding: remaining uncomfortable, thus discounting your ability to do anything about the situation.

Jon tells Alice he is angry at being left to deal with their guests while she was chatting on the phone. She bites her lip and says nothing.

Frank is faced with a pile of unanswered letters and bills to pay. He just sits there staring at the wall.

Overadaption occurs when you act on your fantasy of what others expect, without checking whether it is real or relevant and don't recognise your own interests.

Arthur was about to leave the office, when he noticed that his boss was working late. He imagined that the boss wanted him to finish writing a report, so he took off his coat and got back to work.

Pat's cat has just died and she is dying to tell someone how she feels, but she doesn't phone her friends because she thinks they'll be too busy.

Agitation is repetitive actions which you imagine will relieve your discomfort, but which are purposeless and ineffective in dealing with the situation, for example pacing the floor, finger-tapping, gritting teeth, saying the same thing over and over, shallow fast breathing, constant sighs, futile arguing.

Incapacitation or violence is a futile discharge of energy, directed inwards or outwards. This usually happens after a build-up of agitation which escalates into a desperate attempt to force someone to do something, like fainting, migraine, getting sick, dangerous driving, losing your temper, getting drunk, smashing things, hitting someone.

There is a difference between these behaviours and conscious activities which involve thinking, i.e. choosing to do nothing, adapting because it is the best thing to do, repeating things as a restful activity, or to practice skill, deciding to give up or be violent (like breaking down a door to get in, or beating a cushion to discharge anger).

Passivity on the other hand, is an invitation for someone else to take responsibility for me and to solve my problems, without my having to do anything: express my need, ask for help, make a specific request. This hooks the not-OK parent of the other person to rescue or persecute me.

Whenever we experience passivity in ourselves or others, it is most uncomfortable, because nothing gets resolved. It is called "unfinished business" in Gestalt therapy. The way to deal with passivity is to think actively about what you need to do or say.

The following diagram shows the realistic alternative to passivity.

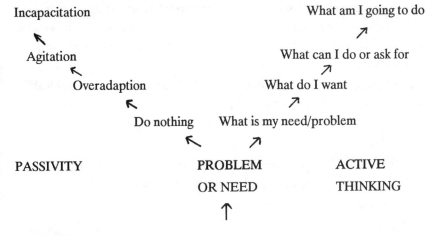

Incapacitation

What am I going to do

Agitation

What can I do or ask for

Overadaption

What do I want

Do nothing   What is my need/problem

PASSIVITY   PROBLEM   ACTIVE
                  OR NEED   THINKING

EXERCISE for self-awareness.

Imagine a situation when you have been passive about a need or problem, i.e. experienced one of the passive behaviours described above.

1) Recall your need, wish, problem or expectation

2) Notice what you actually did

3) Now recall what was the result

4) How did you feel?

Now re-run that scene. This time use the "active thinking" process above to change the outcome.

DRIVERS

Each new situation we find ourselves in, provides us with an opportunity to confirm old patterns or to contradict our script beliefs and change the way we respond.

In Chapter Three we looked at *what* is a person's lifeplan derived mostly from parental injunctions (Don'ts). Now we continue to see *how* we keep the story going.

Whenever we continue to re-enact the past, we reinforce our frame of reference, and discount some aspect of ourselves and/or external reality. A very reliable way to find out how you are discounting - keeping the story going - is to recognise your *drivers*.

One of the most valuable and useful ideas in TA was originated by Taibi Kahler. He identified five basic behaviour patterns (drivers) which covered all the parent messages about *how* we carry out early script decisions and continue the lifescripts.

The five drivers and related script patterns are:

Be Perfect - so I never get it right, I can't make mistakes

Be Strong - so I don't show my feelings,

Try Hard - so I can't finish

Please You - so I always put others first, I don't know how to please myself

Hurry Up - so I don't stop to think where I'm going

Drivers are internal messages - followed by short bursts of energy which we experience whenever we feel uncomfortable. We use the driver to compensate for something that we think is wrong with us. We have a sensation which signals up a slogan about what we are supposed to do next to avoid feeling like that.

Instead of staying in the present, we distort what is actually happening; we ignore options based on reality, and slip into a driver programme - what we are "supposed" to do - and set off to make things "better". This process is based on a faulty frame of reference. The truth is that we make things worse, simply because the signal is a trap which has an inbuilt failure mechanism. For sure, it fills the gap, keeps us going, but it also keeps us not-OK.

Driver behaviour always involves a discount, because it is based on an internal belief that I am only OK if ... (in other words: I must fulfil some condition in order to stay OK). As you may have noticed, this is a Catch 22 situation because, if we have to do something to be OK, we are not OK (being OK is unconditional).

Being OK is not a feeling, a thought, or an action. It is a basic attitude towards yourself. So strictly speaking, it is not true to say "I feel OK" or "I think I'm OK" or that "I do OK things". I AM OK. Either I believe it or not. It is a fundamental reality which sometimes I experience, and sometimes I don't.

Drivers can be recognised by two *internal* factors which only the person experiencing the driver knows:

> physical sensations
>
> internal discounts

There are five other observable clues:

> 1) words (sentence patterns)
>
> 2) tone of voice (and tempo)
>
> 3) physical gestures
>
> 4) body postures
>
> 5) facial expressions

Driver Behaviours

Can you recognise from the chart on the next page what is your primary and secondary driver? No one clue will indicate a driver. You need a cluster. Take care not to judge yourself. Remember: these are descriptions, not judgements - to give you some indication of how you keep telling your story, again and again and again.

For example, if I keep qualifying everything I say or do with a shrug or a "just" (Be Perfect), and I do that dozens of times a day, no wonder I believe I'll never make it!

Driver Behaviors

Driver	Physical Sensation	Internal Discount	Words	Tones	Gestures	Postures	Facial Expressions
Be Perfect	Tense, robotlike	"You should do better"	"of course" "obviously" "efficacious" "clearly" "I think" (tells more than asked)	Clipped, righteous	Counting on fingers, cocked wrist, scratching head	Erect, rigid	Stern, ashamed, embarrassed
Try Hard	Tight stomach, tense shoulders	"You've got to try"	"It's hard" "I can't" "I'll try" "I don't know" (doesn't answer questions—repeats, tangents)	Impatient	Clenched, moving fists	Sitting forward, elbows on legs	Slight frown, perplexed look
Please Me (Someone)	Tight stomach	"You're not good enough"; "Make others feel good"	"You know" "Could you" "Can you" "Kinda" "Um Hmm" "Would you"	High whine	Hands outstretched, head nodding frequently	Head nodding	Raised eyebows, looks away
Hurry Up	Antsy	"You'll never get it done"	"Let's go" (Interrupts people—finishes their sentences)	Up and down	Squirms, taps fingers	Moves quickly	Frowning, eyes shifting rapidly
Be Strong	Numb, rigid	"You can't let them know you're weak"	"No comment" "I don't care" (doesn't use here-and-now feelings)	Hard, monotone	Hands rigid, arms folded	Rigid, one leg over	Plastic, hard, cold

There are no feelings attached to drivers. There is no way to feel a racket without first going through a driver behaviour. Each of these reveal moment-by-moment the story of a person's life. In this way, you keep the story going due to:

1) a low stroke reserve. If you have a low level of positive strokes, and you need a certain number in order to go on living, this has to be made up with negative strokes, which leads you into

2) driver behaviour. You will be more inclined to go into *not-OK* driver behaviour if you have a low stroke count. This is why people play games, get stuck in bad feelings, thoughts or situations.

If a person changes driver-formed *behaviour* sentences, he may change his whole life *process* script pattern.

When you move into a driver, there are a number of possible consequences:

opening the gate to a familiar bad feeling (racket)

the start of a game

an invitation to make a script response (the same or complementary driver)

return to nonscripty behaviour

switch to another driver

escalate into another racket feeling and then

move into anti-script behaviour

or into the final pay-off

Driver Profiles

Developing the idea of driver behaviour, we can see that people tend to display characteristics associated with their major driver, so we can easily recognise five personality types and what they need in order to move into being OK.

BE PERFECT has to get things right, strives for perfection, tends to be very judgmental about people's behaviour. They are ideal computer programmers, engineers and administrators. Most often Be Perfect persons come from a strict or religious family, where right and wrong were set out in very clear and rigid terms, often accompanied by threats or punishments. This kind of person needs permission to make mistakes, to know what is good enough and to be able to accept others, though they may not be perfect.

The **BE STRONG** person is driven by the fear of weakness and therefore has to be self-sufficient for strokes. Brought up where it was a virtue not to let on what you felt or where feelings were scary or oppressive, where expressing emotions was not on, especially not in public. This type has incredible self-control - just the sort of companion for emergencies. Be Strong people need to be encouraged to ask for things. They want relief from their lonely position, and they need getting close to be seen as an acceptable risk.

TRY HARDERS are workaholics. As long as they are working hard, fine. Whether they are achieving anything is secondary. Often they will have 101 unfinished projects going at a time. This driver is like running up an escalator going down. It's all about fear of failure. So they need permission to succeed, to know when to stop, and to get strokes for *being* rather than *doing*.

PLEASERS are the world's great rescuers. They love being helpful and can't bear anyone to be uncomfortable. They control others emotionally by being indispensable. They are nice to everyone, and conform like chameleons to any situation. They are great at serving the public. Unfortunately they always put themselves last and feel frustrated, misunderstood. It is hard to know what the Pleaser really thinks or feels. The permission needed is to please themselves and to know what they really want and feel.

HURRY UP people are living at least two lives at once, feeling close to the edge of death. They will be doing six tasks, while most people feel stretched coping with two. They leave one meeting early in order to get to the next late. They are very competent, busy people who can't stay still. The message in childhood was "Don't just sit there, do something!" Home was either frenetic, chaotic or constantly moving. Hurriers need to be told that there's time to think about what they are doing or that they can stick around long enough to belong in a way that suits them.

PAYOFFS AND ENDINGS

Stories have a beginning, a middle and an ending. There are sub-plots and diversions, but there are clues all the way through as to the likely outcome.

The story of your life is just the same.

In the preceding chapters we have examined the various structures of Transactional Analysis which help us to recognise the life story which we have written, and the patterns of thoughts, feelings and behaviour that limit our options. Some aspects of our lives are free from scripting, other aspects which are predictable are open to change. Whatever we may do with our time, energy and the resources of our personality, it is vital that we pay attention to where we're going.

People often change a behaviour, partner, job or country and in therapy they can make changes without recognising they are still on the same road with the same destination. It is not so important to change what you are doing, but how you're doing your life, because to a great extent it is that which determines the outcomes of each encounter, incident, interaction, episode.

So now I invite you to look where you're going. How does it end for you? What are the *pay-offs* from drivers, games, rackets, and the final script pay-off?

In the previous section we saw how *drivers* have a moment by moment possibility of a not-OK pay-off of going into a racket feeling which in turn can confirm a script belief that when things go wrong I am bound to finish up feeling bad. There is always the possibility of responding to bad things in an OK way so that I can think clearly about options.

If I respond to criticism, for example, by feeling frustrated for not getting it right, I can then move into the vengeful position and stay angry with others or go straight to the final miniscript pay-off of feeling useless or hopeless. Instead I could decide to accept that I got it wrong or didn't match up to someone's standards, and not continue to feel bad. Taibi Kahler asserts that in these moment by moment decisions we are rehearsing the script ending.

The purpose of *racket* feelings is to manipulate people into giving us strokes for feeling bad. If, however, the strokes supply is withdrawn, people then move into playing games. The racket produces a need to make up the stroke quotient. This means that if a person doesn't seek strokes by being straight with people, he will escalate into a *game* where he gets at least temporarily, a fresh supply of strokes, even though they are negative.

Unfortunately, this has to be paid for in the bad pay-off from the game. This is another ending which supports the person's script belief about himself or others: "Just as I thought...", "You see, it only goes to prove that..."

QUESTIONS to increase your awareness of the pay-offs in your life.

1. What keeps on "happening " to you?

> Look back over the past few years and see if you can find a repeating pattern: losing jobs or partners, being let down, struggling to make it, always failing, living dangerously.

2. Why does this always happen to you? How do you explain this pattern?

> I'm no good at choices, frightened of taking risks, bad parents, nothing is good enough, I'm just unlucky.

3. What sort of familiar feeling do you have?

> Despair, worthlessness, rage, panic.

4. Now take a look at how you finish up, when things go wrong?

> Do you give up on yourself or others?

> Do you say "That's life" or "I'll find another way".

It is important to recognise how you set yourself up for certain sorts of endings so that you can see where you are going and break the pattern that you maintain by the way you act in the present with your current beliefs and feelings.

So it is possible to recognise the way your life has been heading since you wrote the first page in your early childhood, from the way you live day by day. When you are in your script you are rehearsing, without realising it, the final scene.

A *script pay-off* is the way, as decreed by its parents, that a child will finish up. The answer to the question "What happens to people like you?" gives the nature of the 'final display' that fulfils the script programme. This could be depression, suicide, addiction, murder, violence, psychosomatic illness, breakdown, boredom, worthlessness. Good pay-offs, such as happy marriage, success, lots of friends, are also possible.

Good endings are when people are aiming to live as long as possible. Whatever happens, they will look for the best outcome. They will trust their free child to know what is good for them and have a positive parent to keep them safe so that they can take risks which have a good chance of success. At the same time, they will not be afraid of failure, they won't let themselves get hurt too badly and if they do by some misfortune, they will let themselves feel the pain as a stimulus to restoring a sense of well-being. They are likely to die of old age. They are not afraid of death because they are not afraid of life.

And whenever we experience the bad pay-offs to drivers, rackets and games, we get clues as to the way our lives will end. In his book *Living your Dying*, Stanley Kellerman describes how we can experience death while we are alive.

When the time comes, I will be ready to die

This life is such a pain, there must be an afterlife.

Most people live their dying as they have lived their lives.

Living is movement, another word for it is process

Living your dying is the story of the movement of your life.

Chapter Five

CHANGING THE STORY OF YOUR LIFE

Throughout this book I have shared with you my view of TA and how it can help you to understand the way you have written the story of your life and throw some light on aspects of your personality and the way you relate to people. There is, in the very language of TA, a dynamic for change. At times you may have thought that it focuses too much on the negative side of experience. That is because TA is concerned to help people recognise what they are doing that is uncomfortable - but with the definite belief that they can change.

First it is important to clarify what is meant by change. All things change. The one predictable thing about life is change. Out of our immediate awareness perhaps we are constantly changing: physically, mentally and emotionally. We are subject to continual change in the material and natural world around us. The question in our personal lives is who is in charge of the change. Ultimately you are not in control of much outside yourself, but you are responsible for your change and how you change.

In his writings Eric Berne talked a lot about *cure*. This is not based on the medical model of cure, though I am sure that as a doctor he thought that mental and emotional problems would be as accessible to treatment as physical complaints. He believed that people could get well without going through long analysis. He once said he was tired of case discussions which were all about trying to explain why patients did not get better. He was adverse to what he called the "subjunctive" approach to therapy: using words which are conditional such as might, could, maybe, if, which prevent people from getting where they are going.

He regarded "making progress" as a counter to changing the script. Essentially he saw cure as the way in which client and therapist agreed to work on a specific problem with a specific goal in sight. This he called making a contract. This is concerned with the emotional and mental process which includes the practicalities of time, fees and responsibility

So TA therapists are committed to change - cure, problem-solving, getting out of script, avoiding games, being aware of rackets, giving, receiving, and asking for as many strokes as you need, using all your ego states, giving up old outdated beliefs, choosing to live the best way for you with regard to others, being creative, spontaneous and intimate.

"Anyone can change and stop the endless struggling, the hassling, the self-caused misery. You can do that by taking charge of your own life."

(William Holloway, *Change Now*, 1973).

Underwriting all this is the belief that everyone is born OK. In practice I describe the experience of loving yourself as the emotional connection with the essential fact that YOU ARE OK.

I may do silly things, harbour evil thoughts or feel rotten, but I AM OK whatever I think or feel or do. My experience tells me that until and unless people recognise this in some way any change is likely to be spurious.

In working with people I seek to corner them into OKness by not letting them use any excuse for rejecting themselves.

By OKness I mean that I am essentially of value, my life has worth, my existence is important to me, and that deep down it is this attitude to myself which governs what I do and how I do it. The vital first step in change is cutting out the internal negative Critical Parent messages which have no place or use to me. While I am constantly judging or blaming myself, I will never change or enjoy life.

Whenever I see people doing this, I get angry with that part of them (for them). You don't have to take that shit - which has been passed on by the not OK part of your parents' Child.

99

So what is this "change?" It is not pure will-power. Adult reasoning is not enough. Learning the facts will only get you so far. Greater adaptation will not achieve any change in script - something all therapists need to be watchful of - changing one adaptation for another.

Essentially we need to re-experience the past and become as little children in order to experience it the way you want to, so that you live in the present likewise.

This approach to TA therapy is called *redecision* as taught and practised by Bob and Mary Goulding. It is basically the way that I work as a therapist. I see that redecision is something that can be experienced outside of therapy - whenever people face a critical moment in their life, which is usually in the company of another who gives the person permission to do something new.

I am regularly asked the question by both my clients and students - is it possible for someone to *change their personality*? My immediate response is usually: "Why would you want to, you're unique?" At a more thoughtful and profound level, I think it is possible for people to make quite profound changes in the way they think or feel or behave. Taking my own experience, before I went into therapy I had a severely depressive personality. My Christian belief enabled me to rise above the disturbance and distress that I always felt. I thought my feelings about myself were accurate - I was bad (sinful), only the grace of God could save me. Leaving the church was a release from a morbid view of life, although on the surface I looked a cheerful, successful family man. It took a long time for me to find my true self and cherish me for who I am. Through my experience in various forms of therapy I eventually decided to give up depression as a way of getting through life.

I remember on the last day of my training with the Gouldings in California saying how good I felt for clearing out so much of the past, but still just wondered if there was a little black cloud that might need dealing with. Mary laughingly said: "Eric, you have spent seven years in therapy and the only thing I can see you suffer from is a slight overdose of introspection!" That was that. Sure I get depressed from time to time, but I no longer suffer from depression. I take it with a pinch of salt. I think my humour and positive approach to people and life is genuine. I no longer have any attachment to digging around. I get angry easily (after ten years of marriage without ever raising my voice). I feel sad about what I've left behind. I do not scare easily.

I accept the sort of person I am, I like my life. I rarely do things I don't want to do. In short, I see myself as quite different from 20 years ago.

So I think that, although the basic personality we have is constant, the way we do and feel about it can change considerably. So often I meet people who have a distorted view of themselves. By focusing on specific changes over a period of time other parts are affected indirectly so that they can be happy and unhappy. Feeling good is normal. Feeling bad is a temporary distress signal that something needs attention, so that you can return to feeling good again. Being happy is a state of mind, not a feeling. It's OK for me to feel miserable. I don't have to judge life through the filter of my misery. So much for changing personality.

Another view about change is TA is what is described as the *integrated Adult*. The Child and Parent ego states are regarded as archaic parts of the personality and the aim of therapy is to help the client to filter the material in the other ego states through the Adult ego state. This can have the effect of denying the validity of experiencing and expressing the distinctive and positive attributes of the personality to feel and care for and about self and others. I do not care for the notion of only transacting from Adult.

The remainder of this chapter is devoted to describing *how* you can change the story of your life. The approach of TA provides a wide spectrum of ways to help people change.

THE START

When a person comes for the help, the TA therapist will seek to establish six basic pieces of information, which he will usually share with the client, so that he can help himself in the process of change.

    1. Messages from parents

    2. Recurring life patterns

    3. The way he experiences his feelings

4. His basic attitude to himself and others

5. Personality structure

6. Behaviour which causes him discomfort

Example of an initial session

A woman comes to a session, unable to be close. Her mother was well educated but never fulfilled her career. She was always around. Her father spent a lot of time away on business. He was strict and punished the children severely. Everyone was polite but little affection was expressed. So her pattern with men was to be successful so that they wouldn't go away. She feared being trapped like her mother. She is cheerful, rarely sad. Never angry. She sees herself as a failure, scared of people in authority and unable to make commitments in her personal life. She cares a lot about others, but keeps aloof and is unaware of her needs. Apart from her work which involves a lot of travelling, she spends most of the time on her own, except when she visits a boy friend in Aberdeen once a month.

At this initial stage I rarely do any direct therapy work. I often give some feedback and usually the process of finding out how you come to be the way you are is enlightening.

As the sessions proceed, I am asking -

Who and What is controlling this person?

What are her messages from the past?

What was her response to her early experience - how did she adapt then, what is troubling her now?

What in her original feelings, desires has been lost, covered up in order to survive?

What information does this person need in order to change?

How does she act out her life pattern *(script)* in her everyday transactions in the present?

The early sessions will be to help the client

1. establish the problem

2. identify the need for change

3. define a goal that can be observed

4. discover the blocks to solving the problem

5. make a mutually acceptable therapeutic contract

There are three possible areas of change - feelings, beliefs and behaviour. Whichever area a client wishes to change - the other two are bound to be affected. When a person comes into therapy I find it useful to establish which area is available for change. It is important to recognise that people feel safer in one mode than others. It is no use trying to work directly at a feeling level with someone who rarely expresses emotion - he is too defended, even though that's what he may have come for.

CONTRACTS FOR CHANGE

In therapy life the first and most important thing to establish is *what* you want to change. TA calls this making a *contract*. This is a major feature of TA therapy. A therapeutic contract is a person's commitment to change something specific. This requires the agreement of the therapist. Many people are vague about change: "I want to be happy, get on better with my partner, improve my self-image ..."

Immediately the task of the therapist is to assist the client to be clear, so that he knows what he might do to help. It is easy to collude with a "forever" contract. With people who have a general dissatisfaction with life, I often suggest a self-awareness contract for a limited period. Often people know very little about themselves and find it hard to discover what is actually wrong.

Others are quite clear about what they want to change. "I want to stop being frightened to talk to people, and express my ideas in public." Although this is a contract for social change, the person is aware that she also needs to deal with her feelings of scare. The point about a contract is that the therapist will focus on the desired change, not on what he thinks is needed.

He may tell the person if he doesn't know, what might be involved in achieving his contract.

There are some contracts which are not valid for a number of reasons:

They are made on behalf of another person

The contract is to please someone else in reality or fantasy.

They'll like me.

I ought to change.

I'm bad.

Unless people really want to change, they won't. That means their Free Child must be involved.

Here is a checklist that I use to help people make a valid contract.

You could use it as follows. Think about something in your life which bothers you. Maybe some small thing that you can easily change. Now go on and answer the questions, then see how you get on during the coming day or week. If you are successful think of something a bit more difficult. If you fail, go back and check the questions again to see where you missed something, for example how long it was going to take you.

What do you want to change? If you change, what will you be doing differently?

How are you going to do it (in and out of the group)

How are you going to make it pay for you? (Consult your Free Child)

How are you likely to sabotage yourself?

What are you going to give up?

Are you *really* going to do it? Yes/No

(A contract is not a wish or something you *should* do)

How will you and I know you've done it?

How long will it take you?

Cure, in my view is when a person has completed his contract. This is likely to involve changing the script, but not necessarily becoming script-free. Eric Berne intimated that complete autonomy is an illusion. Most people go through their lives quite happily, without changing their script. I see that people come into therapy when their script has "run out", become obsolete, doesn't fit anymore, because their experience of life has pushed them to the point where they need to find some new way of life.

SAFETY CONTRACTS - Closing the Escape Hatches
The first essential step before working on a contract is to ensure that your life is safe - that there are no self-destruct buttons waiting to be pushed. It is easy to see that when a person thinks: "Well, if the worst happens, then I can always kill or harm myself or others, or go crazy" - these escapes from life must be dealt with before anyone starts to change. Otherwise there will always be the chance that if it gets too hard, a client may do harmful things or be frightened that he might.

The diagram below based on Franklin Ernst's "OK Corral" demonstrates the four basic life positions that people adopt. The escape hatches are the extreme options of the not-OK positions. *Closing the escape hatches* helps clients to make their lives safe and move towards the I'm OK, You're OK position.

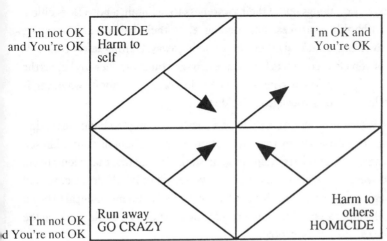

These three exit routes from life have varying levels of harm depending on the extent of a person's not-OKness of self or others.

Examples:

1) Suicide - taking excessive risks which threaten safety - damage to health - letting people walk over you
2) Homicide - violence - reckless behaviour - abuse - putting people down
3) Go crazy - getting drugged out of your mind - losing control - stop thinking

It is no use working on a problem or a need for change while there is any serious ambivalence about whether living itself is worthwhile. If there is any doubt, then this must be worked through first. The simple formula is to get a person to agree not to do anything to harm himself or others or to go crazy. This is a decision for the client, not a promise to the therapist.

Some therapists think that these sort of contracts can be counter-productive - forcing the client into an adaption. It is important to stress that safety contracts must be made with a person's Adult - so that he will monitor his thoughts, feelings and behaviour in such a way that will prevent a tragic outcome. I would not go so far as some TA therapists however and insist that every escape hatch is closed completely forever. That borders on Be Perfect driver behaviour which is bound to push the client into Try Hard or Please You.

People actively do things out of their awareness to maintain a not-OK position. Such as withholding strokes; not looking after their basic needs - eating, sleeping; avoiding, attacking others; and running away. Getting safety contracts and working on clear contracts for change can take time, but therapy begins the moment a client makes a commitment to do something about whatever is bothering him. It takes courage to decide to change.

So these early confrontations are vital if a person is going to change his script. The therapist confronts from a caring position when the client discounts himself - supporting what is good, stroking the small steps. Often I find that clients begin to change when they realise that what they are doing is self-destructive and actively begin to do something different, even if it feels a bit mechanical to begin with. Small shifts can produce large results, even before we begin work on the script issue or presenting problem.

In the early stages of working with people, I use a number of the basic interventional approaches of TA.

1. Recognition of the content of ego states and supporting the Child feelings that have been neglected

2. Strengthening a good internal Parent

3. Helping people to think clearly and face the reality of their life

4. Recognition of obstacles to change

The main method in my work, however, is the process of *redecision*

REDECISION

In order to change the story of your life, you have to re-write it. By that I do not mean that you can change the past, but you can re-experience the past as you are living it out in the present, and change the way you regard the events; change the way you feel about yourself and others; and decide to live the way you choose. As I have indicated above, this kind of change cannot be achieved through insight alone. Knowing how you wrote the story will stimulate painful feelings which have kept you stuck.

Breaking through these bad feelings is the heart of redecision. They are called *impasses* caught between two conflicting options:

One: to stay where you are and follow the programme of your script

The other the desire to be free, which involves confronting habitual ways of thinking and feeling and acting and moving through to a new experience.

A person goes into a room full of people. He wants to talk to them but is scared of rejection. He hovers between keeping away and making contact. He says to himself: "I don't want to be rejected". Another part says: "I don't want to feel left out". If he takes the risk, he has broken through the impasse of his fear. If he backs off, he has broken through the impasse in favour of keeping safe, at least for the time being till the next time.

TWO EXAMPLES

The following examples will illustrate the process.

Phil breaks out of script and changes the programme.

Julia continues the programme but changes the way she feels.

PHIL has been experiencing painful conflicts with his wife. He now realises that he cannot get on with his interests because he is scared of her leaving if he doesn't please her. When he was young, his mother was always ill and constantly in need of attention, so he decided that it was better to take care of her than lose her (she might die). The only advantage he could see in his present behaviour was that his wife depended on him for support. So he was able to re-affirm his contract: to choose what to do when others want him to give up his needs to keep them happy. So then I set up the early scene.

THERAPIST: "You are seven, and your mother has just come home from hospital. Imagine she is lying on that cushion and tell her what you're feeling."

PHIL: "I'm glad you're back. Don't go away again. I'll do anything to stop that. I know you can't look after me, so i'll look after you."

THERAPIST: "You're happy now?"

PHIL: "Not really. I can't go our to play or read books because I have to keep popping in to see if she's alright."

THERAPIST: "Tell her."

PHIL: "I want to go out and play with the boys."

THERAPIST: "What does she say? Be her." *(Phil is then directed to sit on the cushion which represents his mother)*

PHIL: *(as his mother)* "Oh alright, but don't be long. You know I'm very ill."

PHIL: "So I don't go out. I feel too worried about her. She might die."

THERAPIST: "So you're stuck."

PHIL: "Yea." *(he sits frowning for a while)*

THERAPIST: "What are you feeling now?"

PHIL: "Sad *(long pause)* and angry. I've been looking after you like that for years *(he yells)* and I wish you'd die."

THERAPIST: "You want to kill her?"

PHIL: "Well, at least she'd stop scaring me. No, no not really. But I want you to take care of ME."

THERAPIST: "That's a terrible bind you're in. Either which way you lose?"

PHIL: "No, because she wasn't always so ill."

THERAPIST: "OK, so see yourself going up to her room and telling her what you want."

PHIL: *(hesitatingly)* "I want you to tell me that you love me and that I can go out to play without worrying about you."

THERAPIST: "Be your mother and answer."

PHIL: *(as mother)* "Yes, I do love you. Of course you can go out to play as long as you don't go too far."

PHIL: "Damn you. I deserve better than that."

THERAPIST: "Tell her I'm going out and having fun."

PHIL: "Oh no. That would be cruel. You are not supposed to have fun when your mother is suffering."

THERAPIST: "Really? So you have to go on looking after her and be un-happy?"

Members of the group then started to say "Don't let her do that to you."

PHIL: "OK. So Mum, I'm going to play. I can't stop you dying."

THERAPIST: "Now turn from your mother to your wife."

PHIL: "I'm going to enjoy myself with these people even if you're unhappy."

The change with Phil was immediate. He had broken through the impasse. He came out of the edge of the group. And whenever his wife had a "bad turn" he could choose to look after her or follow his own interests. When someone makes a redecision, however small, he experiences release and often surprise. A whole new world opens up. "I didn't know I could do that!"

JULIET is angry with her daughter aged twenty.

JULIET: "You're just wasting your time and fooling around. You do a bit of work to go off to Greece, and now you're back not looking for a job. And I'm supporting you. You've got so much talent. Why don't you ..."

THERAPIST: "So on the one hand you're telling her not to grow up ... and then you get mad that she doesn't. Tell her where you're at."

JULIET: "Damn it, Jane. I'm tired of hauling you out of a mess. I want you to stand on your own two feet."

THERAPIST: "I see, you're damned if you do and damned if you don't. Either you're angry or guilty. You could support her and be happy or refuse and let her find her own way."

JULIET: "Yes, I want to find a way to stop feeling angry at her ... or to stop feeling guilty about saying no."

THERAPIST: "So you're stuck. What was it like when you were her age?"

JULIET: "Oh I was doing secretarial work, and I carried on all through my married life."

THERAPIST: "Was your father alive?"

JULIET: "No, he died in the war, and my mother had to bring us up on her own."

THERAPIST: "OK. Tell her that you're going to fool around for a few years and she can support you."

JULIET: *(starts to cry)* "Oh dear, how I wish. She couldn't support herself."

THERAPIST: "Well I guess that a lot of us would like to have stayed little, so we live out that wish through our kids. Don't worry, I'll take care of everything, and they stay babies and we resent them."

JULIET: "OK, I guess if Jane had my mother, she would have had to look after herself, like I did and not have much fun.

I don't think I was a good mother, and I've been trying to make up for that. I'll stop feeling angry and feel happy to give her money."

In this case, it was not necessary to re-enact the past, neither did Juliet change her way of dealing with her daughter, but she felt OK about what she was doing. She didn't change her script, just learned to accept it and not feel bad.

Redecision is primarily a shift in the Child ego state. The Little Professor made the early decision which was the best he could do at the time.

So it is that part of the Free Child that can find another way now, with increased power and knowledge of his Parent and Adult. It involves a change in all three ego states. The purpose of redecision is to change the outcome of the early scene, so that the client can reclaim his lost feelings and sense, gain release from the power of the parents' negative messages (injunctions) and take in new permissions to choose.

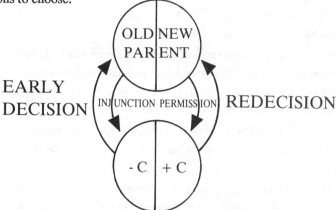

Sometimes people have to visit the scene a number of times before they are willing to break through and allow themselves to re-experience the Free Child feelings that they shut down in order to get through and conform to the early injunction. They need to have the courage to take the risk of moving away from a comfortable but unhappy state.

When the emotional shift has taken place, three things are important.

    1. Anchoring the experience by practising the new decision in the group

    2. Practising something new outside the group. How are you going to be different now?

    3. A good enough internal Parent. (Sometimes this self-reparenting needs to take place before moving into redecision)

Now I will describe briefly how I conduct self-reparenting. It doesn't always take place in this structured way, but usually all the elements are present.

SELF REPARENTING

The timing of this technique is vital and varies with each client, but it is rarely effective at an early stage of therapy, because a client usually doesn't have enough idea of the content of his ego states.

The primary factor is awareness of need (Child) and a lack of internal parenting. A person may be lonely, depressed, scared, guilty but have no idea that they can do anything about it. Quite often they are living passively, hoping that something or someone will "happen".

Sometimes it is helpful to do a bit of teaching about the Parent ego state, how it is full of a lot of negation messages about a person's worth, abilities and needs which can be replaced with helpful ones.

It can be most useful in supporting a new decision. Phil would need to find inside himself the mother he lacked to take care of his need to enjoy himself.

It is aimed at getting a client to find new resources inside himself, so that he can support himself and not unrealistically depend on others. Often people will be feeling a bit of anger at the way the world is for them. I have also noticed that it can be a way of opening up Child feelings which have been ignored or avoided.

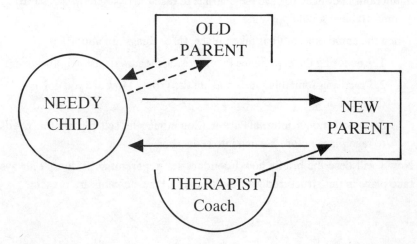

A chair and a cushion are arranged facing each other, with another chair and a cushion on either side

I act as coach tot he New Parent and only give stage directions to the Needy Child.

THERAPIST: "Margaret, sit on the cushion and be your Needy Child. Imagine your ideal parent is sitting on the chair listening to you. It may help to think of someone who is like the mother or father you wanted. Now talk to her about how you feel and difficulties you have right now."

MARGARET: "I am feeling very sad. I don't know what to do. I'm fed up with my husband being so stressed that he gives me nothing. I feel unloved, I'm always taking care of everyone. No-one seems to care about me."

THERAPIST: "Now move the chair. Be your good Parent, that part of you that is capable and understanding. Talk to Margaret."

MARGARET: *(as Parent)* "Well, I can see that you are miserable. I wish I could help you."

THERAPIST: "Tell her that you love her."

MARGARET: *(as Parent)* "I love you" *(she breaks down sobbing)*.

THERAPIST: "Move back to the cushion and tell her why you're crying."

MARGARET: "How can you love me? I can't bear it. You never did."

THERAPIST: "I think you are now talking to your real mother. Tell her." *(I point to the other chair)*

MARGARET: "You never took any notice of me. You gave so much to Gill" *(her sister)*.

It may be necessary at times to let the dialogue between the Child and the old Parent go on a bit, until there is some movement.

MARGARET: "I want you to look at me."

THERAPIST: "It's too late. Talk to your good Parent."

She does so and then I get her back into the New Parent chair and say:

THERAPIST: "Now tell her again that you love her, without crying - that's her tears, not yours."

MARGARET: *(as Parent)* "I do love you. I think you're important. But you mustn't worry. Everything will be alright."

THERAPIST: "That sounds like her old mother. Tell her whatever happens, you'll always be there for her."

She does so. Then I direct her to the Child cushion and get her to repeat what she has heard her good Parent saying. When she does this, her face lights up.

MARGARET: "I think you mean it".

This is a brief glimpse at this method. It takes time and fine tuning from the therapist to recognise quickly where the internal transactions are misdirected. And a vast supply of potential and accurate coaching from the therapist's Parent, and an ability to recognise negative Parent messages. Though old stuff may come up, its important to get it out and get back to the new parenting quickly.

At first it can seem a bit artificial, until the client realises how much power he has given to the old voices and shut down on getting his needs met. Mostly though people report profound changes when they listen to the new messages and discover a good mother or father inside them.

It is helpful to ensure that the client finds a way of using his New Parent to get some nurture from the group.

GROUPS

TA therapy is essentially a group method, and is most effective in this setting. For various reasons some clients prefer working individually and most TA therapists provide this alternative: the group intensive which lasts two or more whole days. There is much to recommend this, particularly in a residential setting where much of the redecision and changes can be experienced within a supportive community away from the pressures of daily life which often collude with a person's script.

In the final section of this book on my approach to therapy, I describe how I work generally with groups.

Chapter Six

MY APPROACH TO THERAPY

The conviction that inspires my work is the belief that people can change, and that life is essentially good. For the most part, I like the people I work with, and enjoy the mutual enrichment and learning involved in being a therapist. Using Transactional Analysis as a framework, I make the kind of relationships with my clients which will help them to understand themselves better, so that they can make realistic choices in their lives.

TA provides a clear structure for working with people. At the same time it helps me to maintain a clear focus on what I am doing. It relieves me from having to be right. When I make a mistake, that can be part of the process of finding out what is happening in the relationship. If I stand back too much, I can express my reluctance to intervene and talk about whether I am being over- protective. If I become over-active, we can look at what is going on between us that is causing me to do so much work. I can check if I am too caring or not giving enough direction (Parent). Without making judgements, I am able to recognise my feelings and see if they fit.

What I like most about TA is its flexibility. I can find a place for a variety of techniques and insights from other methods. Within TA there are a wide range of emphases, from analytical to body work. My approach derives much from my early training in Gestalt therapy and later with Bob and Mary Goulding who practice a TA/Gestalt approach which they call redecision therapy, which I have described in Chapter Five.

One of the major tools in TA is the therapeutic contract - what a person wants to change. I work with three different kinds of contract for change:

1) Self-awareness - a client will need to discover and understand what kind of person he is, how he relates to others in different situations. In a group a lot of this work can be done in the here and now.

2) Social change - re-structuring the way a client uses his time and energy, which involves some resolution of internal (Parent-Child) conflicts.

3) Emotional change - gaining release from difficult feelings or destructive behaviour.

One of my initial attractions to TA was its origins in groupwork. I work mainly in groups, as they provide for a more normal environment for change than one-to-one therapy. People experience a range of different responses in addition to the therapist's, which frees me from being in sharp focus the whole time, and discourages over-dependence on the therapist. I think it also gives a lot of mutual protection, support and time for members to learn while others are working. They can be as active as they wish. In a group I can see more clearly how people interact with others, and use the group for experimenting with new behaviour. The advantage of individual therapy is that the client has the undivided attention of the therapist for the whole session, and this allows for a wider range of issues to be dealt with, though not necessarily in greater depth.

There are three factors which I take into account in deciding to work individually with clients:

a) Unsuitability for a group due to the nature of the problem or because this might be disruptive.

b) The client is unable to attend a group due to more important commitments.

c) The client expresses a strong preference to work individually.

However, I usually put a strong case at the interview for joining a group, particularly when a person has problems about relating. Group members do have the option of individual sessions occasionally as the need arises. Quite often individual clients join a group at a later stage.

I see myself primarily as a group therapist, mainly because I enjoy the interaction. For me, individual therapy is usually harder work and I have to limit the number of weekly sessions to avoid overload. In addition I think TA works far better in a group - it is transactional.

Every prospective client has an interview without obligation, to elicit vital information. For this I use a short series of questions to get a clear picture of the problem: how he came to be the way he is (elements of his script), an outline of important life events, any physical problems or previous therapy. It is important for us to have a workable contract. Do we both feel comfortable about working together? I am not happy working with anyone who is alcoholic or a drug user, nor those who have a history of violence, unless I am satisfied that they have or are willing to agree not to resort to physical damage. I remember two people I refused to work with, one who coolly told me that she had stabbed her husband without remorse and another who, late at night, drove his car into roundabouts at 100 mph. If there is evidence of suicidal tendencies, that is the first thing I work on. TA insists on safety contracts as being essential to effective therapy. Occasionally I have declined to work with someone because his problem or situation is too close to me at the time. Although I have had clients who suffer from extreme personality disorders with episodes of psychotic breakdown, I usually refer these to therapeutic communities. Occasionally I will send those with serious disturbance to a psychiatric colleague for his diagnosis. Generally speaking, the people who come to me are experiencing emotional or social difficulties without being seriously dysfunctional - at a basic level they can manage their lives.

The basic language of TA is understood by members of my groups. If they do not have any knowledge, I give them a booklet or they can attend an introductory workshop. This is of great value in helping clients to be aware of how they enact their problems in their daily lives. They start to identify the difference they experience being in Parent, Adult or Child, and notice the games they play to act out their beliefs about themselves. It also enables them to incorporate the changes they make in therapy outside the group.

The process that I commonly use consists of the following elements:

My groups are on-going. They meet every week through the year, except for holidays. They form my primary therapeutic work.

After a round of sharing news and what they've been doing about their contracts, members take time to do personal work on what they want to change.

So the members set their own "agenda". Usually they will work directly with me, though others are encouraged to intervene. Apart from this, I rarely offer any structures. People take responsibility for how they use the time. No-one *has* to work, although I may ask why someone is not sharing, or leaving himself out. At the end of their first session I usually ask new members to tell us how they experienced the group.

I work with whatever people bring up related to their contract, or issues that need urgent attention. In this, I draw on a range of resources appropriate to their needs - Gestalt, dreamwork, dialogues, with parts of themselves or others involved in their lives, re-enactment of family scenes, self-reparenting, creative visualisation, role play and body awareness.

My first objective is to give space for people to express their needs. We don't waste time with generalities. As soon as someone shares a need or difficulty, I ask him to be specific about when and how he experiences it and what he wants to change. After reporting this from his Adult. I probe for the feelings which may be blocking a person. As soon as possible I get him to express directly what is happening by "talking" to the person concerned, or a part of him which is causing trouble.

Although I work in groups, my interest in group dynamics is limited. The purpose of my groups is to help individuals solve their problems, and only when interpersonal conflicts get in the way of this do I allow space to deal with them. I use the process to show what may be blocking a person in changing. The group can be used for checking out what people imagine others are thinking or feeling about them, to confront games and to affirm members when they take a new step in achieving their contract.

My style of therapy is inter-active. I am involved as a person, and share my thoughts and feelings without pressure. I invite people to be themselves. Although I will occasionally push people, I avoid getting them to do anything they don't want to. If they are resisting, I often go along with it until they are ready to move. Sometimes I will trick them into a direction I know they want to go in and tell them. I stop people reciting miseries and failures for the umpteenth time. I stroke them for their power, their clear thinking and resourcefulness, their courage or ingenuity in any change they make. I will comfort them in their pain. I cheer on the little kid in them who somehow found a way to get through, in spite of unhelpful parenting or misfortune.

I am always looking for the old feelings that are often hidden away. One woman constantly scratched her hands when she talked about her mother. I asked her if she was angry and she said: "No, I'm trying to hold on to her - she was always pushing me away". I encourage clients to talk *to* people rather than *about* them - "Be with your father now, and tell me how sad you are that he didn't spend more time with you." I track alongside them asking myself: "What's all this about?" When I am feeling uncomfortable, I will share it when I sense something is fishy.

I am not afraid to tell a person when I strongly dislike what he is doing. I will often stop working with someone without rejecting him, when I think we're going nowhere. Sometimes I get lost, and say so. Sometimes I don't know what's happening and I start to wonder what I'm doing. Occasionally I say something seemingly inappropriate which wakes everyone up (including me!). I have had verbal fights with group members which can be very upsetting, but on reflection something important gets resolved. Usually I am very alert, and while I care about my clients, I do not "behave" myself all the time. I can be devious, teasing, angry, forgetful even. It's not the things I gave or said that bothers me, it's all the things I hid.

Most of what I do is based on the TA concept of early decisions. It doesn't usually take long to find these out by simple questions. I ensure that people do a lot of thinking, until they signal up some feelings. "I was talking to a colleague, when a couple of women came into the office. He turned away and chatted with them and I felt left out". Most therapy starts with ordinary stuff like that.

How do I behave in groups? I don't move much except to direct people, to see them more clearly and make closer contact with them. I use my hands and face a lot to express myself when listening or to emphasise what I am saying. I don't go in for over-dramatic actions. What I do is quiet and purposeful. A client commented: "The group is like ordinary life". To me that means it is not too precious to be applied outside the group.

Apart from my skills, training and knowledge, I see my experience of life as a vital resource. From my life I offer people hope for change.

My object is to get people out of therapy as soon as they have got what they came for. I see therapy largely as a short-term experience to help them to get on with their lives, rather than using it to avoid their predicament.

One of the main aspects of my work is to help people to recognise the difference between pain in the present and that which is related to the past. Rarely it is all one or the other, but if a client experiences great difficulty in changing his present discomfort by taking effective action, then he needs to re-experience the old decision to be unhappy as a protection against something which he imagines to be worse. Healing the past consists of finding ways to make the present good. Therapy is mainly "grief" work, letting go of what was good or bad in the past and is no longer, wishing things were different "if only", and letting go of unreal hopes for the future.

Being in therapy doesn't mean you have to dredge up tons of bad stuff to be dealt with. As soon as a person finds a way to use his energy for being OK, he will drop his old rackets, games and useless (script) beliefs. For me therapy can be fun, and change can be accompanied by laughter and relief.

I appreciate the hundreds of people I have worked with for the variety of ways they have shown me of being human.

BIBLIOGRAPHY

Major books on TA
Eric Berne: *Transactional Analysis in Psychotherapy*. Grove Press 1961

Eric Berne: *Principles of Group Treatment*. Grove Press 1966

Eric Berne: *Games People Play*. Penguin 1968

Eric Berne: *What do you say after you say Hello?* Corgi 1975

Eric Berne: *Sex in Human Loving*. Penguin 1973

Tom Harris: *I'm OK, You're OK*. Pan MacMillan

Graham Barnes: *TA after Eric Berne*. Harper's College Press 1977

Muriel James: *Techniques in TA*. Addison-Wesley 1977

Muriel James & Dorothy Jongeward: *Born to Win*. Addison-Wesley 1971

Claude Steiner: *Scripts People Live*. Bantam 1975

Bob & Mary Goulding: *The Power is in the Patient*. TA Press 1978

Bob & Mary Goulding: *Changing Lives through Redecision Therapy*. Brunner-Mazel 1979

Jacqui Schiff et al: *The Cathexis Reader*. Harper and Row 1975

Ian Stewart & Vann Joines: *TA Today*. Lifespace Publishing, 1987

Ian Stewart: *TA Counselling in Action*. Sage 1989

Other books mentioned in this volume.
Carl Whitaker: *Midnight Musings of a Family Therapist*. Norton & Co. 1989

Stanley Kellerman: *Living your Dying*. Random House. 1974

Elisabeth & Henry Jorgensen: *Eric Berne: Master Gamesman*. Grove Press 1984

Mavis Klein: *Lives People Live*. John Wiley 1980

Jay Haley: *Uncommon Therapy*. Norton & Co. 1986

RESOURCES

ORGANISATIONS

The International Transactional Analysis Association (ITAA)
1772 Vallejo Street, San Francisco, California 94123, USA.
The European Association for Transactional Analysis (EATA)
Case Grand-Pré 59, CH-1211, Geneva 16, Switzerland
The Institute of Transactional Analysis (ITA Great Britain)
BM Box 4104, London, WC1 3XX

PUBLICATIONS

Transactional Analysis Journal - ITAA, Quarterly.
The Script - ITAA, Monthly Newsletter.
Newsletter - EATA, three times a year.
ITA News - ITA, three times a year.
All these are available by becoming a member of the ITA.

TRAINING

Anyone wishing to undertake training in TA is required to take the "101" - the official introduction to TA. Programmes of training and supervision are offered by Certified and Provisional Teaching Members. Those who want to gain accreditation as TA practitioners need to sign a training contract with a Teaching Member. Others can participate in open training events on a non-contractual basis.

Certified Teaching Members

Petruska Clarkson - London W5

Sue Fish - London, W5

Maria Gilbert - London W5

Gordon Law - Malvern, Worcs.

Adrienne Lee - Nottingham

Charlotte Sills - London, W5

Ian Stewart - Nottingham

Alice Stevenson - Sandhurst, Kent

Margaret Turpin - Marlborough, Wilts.

Brenda Tweed - Birmingham

THERAPY

Those seeking professional help with their problems should consult an accredited TA practioner. Details of these and information about TA membership can be obtained by writing to the ITA at the above address.

SELECTED INDEX

Page numbers indicate where the definition or description of the key words in the text are to be found.